Thomas Nicholson

Gems from the States

Song and Sense

Thomas Nicholson

Gems from the States
Song and Sense

ISBN/EAN: 9783744766838

Printed in Europe, USA, Canada, Australia, Japan

Cover: Foto ©Thomas Meinert / pixelio.de

More available books at **www.hansebooks.com**

GEMS FROM THE STATES.

BEING A SECOND SERIES OF

"SONG AND SENSE

FROM

UNCLE SAM."

COLLECTED BY

THOMAS NICHOLSON.

LONDON :

S. W. PARTRIDGE & Co., PATERNOSTER ROW, E.C.

1886.

LONDON

J. C. DURANT, PRINTER, CLEMENT'S HOUSE,

CLEMENT'S INN PASSAGE, W.C.

CONTENTS.

INDEX OF FIRST LINES.

GEMS FROM THE STATES.

DOMESTIC.

THE "COMING MAN."

A PAIR of very chubby legs,
  Encased in scarlet hose ;
A pair of little stubby boots,
  With rather doubtful toes ;
A little kilt, a little coat,
  Cut as a mother can—
And lo ! before us strides, in state,
  The future " coming man."

His eyes perchance will read the stars,
  And search their unknown ways ;
Perchance the human heart and soul
  Will open to their gaze ;
Perchance their keen and flashing glance
  May be a nation's light—
Those eyes, that now are wistful bent
  On some " big fellow's " kite.

That brow, where mighty thoughts will dwell
   In solemn, secret state,
Where fierce Ambition's restless strength
   Shall war with future fate :
Where Science from now hidden caves
   New treasures shall outpour—
Tis knit now, with a troubled doubt,
   Are two, or three, cents more ?

Those lips that, in the coming years,
   Will plead, or pray, or teach ;
Whose whispered words, on lightning flash,
   From world to world may reach ;
That, sternly grave, may speak command,
   Or smiling, win control—
Are coaxing now for ginger-bread
   With all a baby's soul ?

Those hands—those little busy hands—
   So sticky, small and brown ;
Those hands, whose only mission seems
   To tear all order down—
Who knows what hidden strength may lie
   Within their chubby grasp,
Though now tis but a taffy-stick
   In sturdy hold they clasp ?

Ah, blessings on those little hands,
   Whose work is not undone !
And blessings on those little feet,
   Whose race is yet unrun !
And blessings on the little brain
   That has not learned to plan !
Whate'er the future holds in store,
   God bless the " coming man."

MY BABY.

LITTLE allspice, pepper, pickle !
Baby, changeable and fickle,
Lying in your nurse's arms,
Safe from everything that harms.
Full of smiles, and full of tears,
Full of joys, and full of fears,
Are you mortal or divine ?
Tell me, little baby mine !

Little cherub, sunshine, star,
Baby, comfort of mamma,
Welcome to this world with kisses,
Crowned with love and earthly blisses.
Dimpled darling, blue-eyed boy,
A future hope, a present joy ;
Why thus round my heart entwine ?
Tell me, little baby mine !

MY NEW YEAR'S GIFT.

BY AUGUSTA MOORE.

A LITTLE lovely baby boy,
  With features soft and fair ;
With smiles upon his dimpled cheeks,
  And sunshine in his hair.

Sent to me o'er the tossing sea
  From a far sunset shore ;
So that my lonely life may be
  Silent and sad no more.

With kisses on his rosy lips,
  And love within his eyes ;
This is my New Year's treasure bright,
  The present that I prize.

The New Year hath no other gift
  One half so full of joy,
One half so sweet and beautiful
  As my dear baby boy.

A GROWN-UP BIRTHDAY.

BY SUSAN COOLIDGE.

THIS is my birthday, baby. Did you know
  Aunties had birthdays too ?   Why, how you
      stare !
Your wide eyes, like two solemn mountain lakes,
  Set in a fringe of pale, larch-yellow hair.
      " Do they have cakes ? "

No, cakes are not for people old as I ;
  They grow for little folks, the pretty things,
All sweet and pink, with glittering sugar top
  And lighted tapers set in careful wings.
      " When did you stop ? "

A long time since, before our baby came.
  You needn't look so very sorry, dear.
It is no matter ; Auntie doesn't care.
  She has cake every night—not once a year.
      " How old are you ? "

Well, yes.   I used to sit up in a pew
  At church, when I was small like you, and
    stare
At men and women not so old as I,
  And wonder at their wrinkles and gray hair.
      "Why don't you cry?"

Ah! baby, why? How can I tell you that?
  You bloom too near the ground, my violet
    blue,
To look beyond the grass and flowers close by,
  I, taller grown, have further sight than you.
      And see the sky.

Above the vapory mists that shroud the plain—
  Above the further clouds, my vision flies,
To seek the place of the all-perfect day ;
  And fain my feet would follow where my eyes
      Have shown the way.

I climb, and the road widens all the way ;
  I near—the morning breaks, the fog-wreaths
    fly ;
I breathe a heavenly air, and hear at times
  The sound of bell-notes pealing clear and high
      In welcoming chimes.

Each step but brings me nearer to the goal ;
  Each milestone left behind marks one mile
    past ;
Each moment grows the vision on my eyes ;
  Each birthday says :—The end is coming fast.
      Beloved, arise.

What am I saying?   Never mind, my pet,
   Auntie was talking stupid, grown-up talk.
Don't wrinkle so your pretty, puzzled brow
   And try to understand ; but come and walk.
    " I like you now."

A GENTLE HERO.

BY F. D. MASON.

As oft I walk along a quiet street,
   And pass a small white cottage, neat and plain,
   I see a meek, white face pressed to the pane
Of the low window.   Patient eyes I meet,—
Child's eyes that in their purity are sweet.
   Yet in their gaze I see their owner fain
   Would have some gift denied, some boon
    would gain,
Without which life perhaps seems incomplete.
A sufferer for life the gentle boy,
   And still he never murmurs at his fate,
   But like that Spartan lad, the pain he bears,
And smiles as though his sorrow were a joy.
   How many lives there are, sublimely great,
   Of which the world knows not amid its cares !

THE BOY THAT LAUGHS.

BY GEORGE COOPER.

I KNOW a funny little boy,
   The happiest ever born ;
His face is like a beam of joy,
   Although his clothes are torn.

I saw him tumble on his nose,
   And waited for a groan;
But how he laughed!   Do you suppose
   He struck his funny bone?

There's sunshine in each word he speaks,
   His laugh is something grand;
Its ripples overrun his cheeks,
   Like waves on snowy sand.

He laughs the moment he awakes,
   And till the day is done;
The schoolroom for a joke he takes,
   His lessons are but fun.

No matter how the day may go,
   You cannot make him cry;
He's worth a dozen boys I know,
   Who pout, and mope, and sigh.

WHICH LOVED BEST.

BY JOY ALLISON.

" I LOVE you, mother," said little John,
Then, forgetting his work, his cap went on,
And he was off to the garden swing,
And left her the water and wood to bring.

" I love you, mother," said rosy Nell,
" I love you better than tongue can tell,"
Then she teased and pouted full half the day,
Till her mother rejoiced when she went to play.

" I love you, mother," said little Fan,
" To-day I'll help you all I can ;
How glad I am school doesn't keep ! "
So she rocked the babe till it fell asleep.

Then, stepping softly, she fetched the broom,
And swept the floor and tidied the room ;
Busy and happy all day was she,
Helpful and happy as child could be.

" I love you, mother," again they said—
Three little children going to bed.
How do you think that mother guessed
Which of them really loved her best ?

THE BALD-HEADED TYRANT.

BY MARY E. VANDYNE.

O ! THE quietest home on earth had I,
  No thought of trouble, no hint of care ;
Like a dream of pleasure the days fled by,
  And Peace had folded her pinions there ;
But one day there joined in our household band
A bald-headed tyrant from No-man's-land.

O, the despot came in the dead of night,
  And no one ventured to ask him why ;
Like slaves we trembled before his might,
  Our hearts stood still when we heard him cry ;
For never a soul could his power withstand,
That bald-headed tyrant from No-man's-land.

He ordered us here and he sent us there—
  Though never a word could his small lips speak—
With his toothless gums and his vacant stare,
  And his helpless limbs so frail and weak,
Till I cried, in a voice of stern command,
"Go up, thou bald-head from No-man's-land."

But his abject slaves they turned on me;
  Like the bears in Scripture they'd rend me there,
The while they worshipped with bended knee
  This ruthless wretch with the missing hair;
For he rules them all with relentless hand,
This bald-headed tyrant from No-man's-land.

Then I searched for help in every clime,
  For peace had fled from my dwelling now,
Then I finally thought of old Father Time,
  And low before him I made my bow.
"Wilt thou deliver me out of his hand,
This bald-headed tyrant from No-man's-land?"

Old Time he looked with a puzzled stare,
  And a smile came over his features grim.
"I'll take the tyrant under my care:
  Watch what my hour-glass does to him.
The veriest humbug that ever was planned
Is this same bald-head from No-man's-land."

Old Time is doing his work full well—
  Much less of might does the tyrant wield;
But, ah! with sorrow my heart will swell,
  And sad tears fall as I see him yield.
Could I stay the touch of that shrivelled hand,
I would keep the bald-head from No-man's-land.

For the loss of peace I've ceased to care ;
  Like other vassals, I've learned, forsooth,
To love the wretch who forgot his hair
  And hurried along without a tooth.
And he rules me, too, with his tiny hand,
This bald-headed tyrant from No-man's-land.

DO THINGS WELL.

WHATSOEVER you find to do,
  Do it boys with all your might ;
Never be a little true,
  Or a little in the right.
Trifles even
  Lead to heaven,
Trifles make the life of man ;
  So in all things,
  Great or small things,
Be as thorough as you can.

MISCHIEF.

" UNLOCK the bath-room door, baby,
  And let your mamma in ;
What is the water running for,
  And making such a din ? "

" Baby wants mamma go away—
  She can't get in 'e door—
Fo' baby's sailing 'ittle boats
  In rivers on 'e floor ;

" But pretty soon I let 'oo in ;
    An' mamma musn't c'y,—
For baby's took his new blue dress
    An' wiped 'e floor all dry ! "

" The baby's soaked from top to toe !
    The parlour ceiling's wet !
Does this earth hold one single spot
    Where that child cannot get ? "

JINGLES.

WHO can tell what a baby thinks ?
When it wakes from its forty winks,
And rubs its face into numerous kinks,
And stares at the light that comes in at the chinks
Of its rock-a-by nest, and gapes and blinks,
Who can tell what a baby thinks ?

Who has courage to venture a a guess
As to what the baby may think of its dress,
Trimmed and ruffled to such excess ? -
Or what the baby may think of the mess
For headache and toothache and stomach distress,
And for all its ailings, more or less ?

What does it think when it wakes at night,
With all the pretty things out of sight,
With nobody stirring and " making a light ? "
Does it think its condition is far from right,
And that big folks are not at all polite,
And treat their visitors far from right,
And that darkness is meant for a personal slight ?
Is that the reason it takes delight

In screaming with all its personal might,
And rousing the neighbours, at dead of night?

And what do you think that the baby thinks,
Looking about like a mild-eyed lynx,
Watching the spoon that tinkles and clinks,
While papa is warming its catnip drinks,
Over a candle that glimmers and blinks,
Humming and drumming out " Cap'n Jinks,"
That the children skate to, now, at the rinks,
What do you think that the baby thinks?

Did you say that babies are thinkless things,
With no other light than what instinct brings,
With brains as downy as butterflies' wings,
And heads as empty as a bell that swings
Over and under, and rings and sings,
When muscular motion is moving the strings?
Did you say that babies are thinkless things?

Then when does the thing begin to grow?
And when does the mind begin to show?
And when does the baby begin to know
That this is true, or this is so?
Say, when you find out, please let me know!

THE QUEEN IN HER CARRIAGE IS RIDING BY.

O, THE queen in her carriage is passing by :
Her cheeks are like roses, her eyes like the sky ;
Her wonderful teeth are white as new milk,
Her pretty blonde hair is softer than silk.

She's the loveliest monarch that ever was seen ;
You ask of what country the darling is queen ;
Her empire extends not to far distant parts,
She's queen of our household, the mistress of hearts.

For sceptre she lifts her soft dimpled hands ;
Her subjects all hasten to heed her commands ;
Her smile is bewitching, and fearful her frown,
And all must obey when she puts her foot down.

May blessings descend on that bright little head,
From the time she awakes, till she's safely in bed ;
And now do you guess, when I speak of the queen,
'Tis only our six months baby I mean ?

NOBODY'S CHILD.

ONLY a newsboy under the light
  Of the lamp-post, plying his name in vain ;
Men are too busy to stop to-night,
  Hurrying home through the sleet and rain.
Never since dark a paper sold ;
  Where shall he sleep, or how be fed ?
He thinks as he shivers there in the cold,
  While happy children are safe a-bed.

Is it strange if he turns about,
  With angry words, then comes to blows,
When his little neighbour, just sold out,
  Tossing his pennies, past him goes ?
" Stop !"—someone looks at him sweet and mild,
  And the voice that speaks is a tender one ;
" You should not strike such a little child,
  And you should not use such words, my son !"

Is it his anger or his fears
   That have hushed his voice and stopped his
      arm ?
"Don't tremble"; these are the words he hears,
   "Do you think that I would do you harm ?"
"It isn't that," and the hand drops down ;
   "I wouldn't care for kicks and blows,
But nobody ever called me son,
   Because I'm nobody's child, I s'pose."

O men ! as you careless pass along,
   Remember the love that has cared for you ;
And blush for the awful shame and wrong
   Of a world where such a thing could be true !
Think what the child on your knee had been,
   If thus on life's lonely billows tossed ;
And who shall bear the weight of the sin
   If one of these "little ones" be lost !

SONG.

H. W. LONGFELLOW.

STAY, stay at home, my heart, and rest ;
Home-keeping hearts are happiest,
For those that wander they know not where
Are full of trouble and full of care ;
   To stay at home is best.

Weary and homesick and distressed,
They wander East, they wander West,
And are baffled and beaten and blown about
By the winds of the wilderness of doubt ;
   To stay at home is best.

Then stay at home, my heart, and rest ;
The bird is safest in its nest ;
O'er all that flutter their wings and fly
A hawk is hovering in the sky ;
    To stay at home is best.

FANNY'S MUD PIES.

BY ELIZABETH SILL.

UNDER the apple tree spreading and thick,
Happy with only a pan and a stick,
On the soft grass in the shadow that lies,
Our little Fanny is making mud pies.

On her brown apron and bright drooping head
Showers of pink and white blossoms are shed ;
Tied to a branch that seems meant just for that,
Dances and flutters her little straw hat.

Gravely she stirs with a serious look,
" Making believe " she's a true pastry cook ;
Sundry brown splashes on forehead and eyes
Shows that our Fanny is making mud pies.

But all the spoil of her innocent play
Clean soap and water will wash away ;
Many a pleasure in daintier guise
Leaves darker traces than Fanny's mud pies.

Dash, full of joy in the bright summer day,
Zealously chases the robins away,
Barks at the squirrels, or snaps at the flies,
All the while Fanny is making mud pies.

Sunshine and soft summer breezes astir,
While she is busy, are busy with her ;
Cheeks rosy glowing and bright sparkling eyes
Bring they to Fanny while making mud pies.

Dollies and playthings are all laid away,
Not to come out till the next rainy day.
Under the blue of those sweet summer skies
Nothing's so pleasant as making mud pies.

WATCHING FOR PAPA.

BY ANNIE D. WARE.

SHE always stood upon the steps,
    Just by the cottage door,
Waiting to kiss me, when I came
    Each night home from the store.
Her eyes were like two glorious stars,
    Dancing in Heaven's own blue ;
" Papa," she'd call, like a wee bird,
    " I's lootin' out for you."

Alas ! how sadly do our lives
    Change as we onward roam ;
For now no birdie voice calls out
    To bid me welcome home.
No little arms stretch out to me,
    No blue eyes, dancing bright,
Are peeping from the cottage door,
    When I come home at night.

And yet, it comforts me to think
  That when I'm called away,
From scenes below, to those of bright
  And everlasting day,
A little angel at the gate,
  With eyes divinely blue,
Will call with birdie voice, " Papa,
  I's lootin' out for you."

THE MOTHER'S LEGACY.

BY MRS. S. T. PERRY.

CHILDREN, the sun is almost down—
  How very clear the western sky !
Before the dew begins to fall,
  We'll have a talk here, you and I.
I've watched the sun set, from this porch,
  Day after day, many a year ;
Sometimes it went down in a cloud,
  But oftener the sky was clear.

We're apt to think life's full of clouds,
  But there's more sunshine on the whole ;
We lose so much of it because   .
  We close the windows of the soul.
Although we may have warmth and light,
  We will persist in shade to dwell,
And find out, when it is too late,
  We could have sunshine just as well.

C

Perhaps you think it strange I call
   You children still, but don't you know
That little ones, in mother's heart,
   Never to men and women grow ;
I cannot think, John, you have passed
   Your fortieth birthday, but 'tis true—
Why, yes, and more, if you should live
   'Till April, you'll be forty-two !

You have been married twenty years,
   My Sarah, and are thirty-nine.
Who can believe it possible ?
   Alas, how very fast goes time !
And Willie, if he were alive,
   Just wait a minute—let me see ;
'n eighteen fifty he was born—
   Yes, that will make him twenty-three.

Some people think that children grow
   In heaven, but I never could.
If Willie is not still a child,
   The meeting won't seem half so good.
And, ever since he went away,
   There's been the mercy in the cup,
To think, when I get home, I'll have
   One child that never will grow up.

Poor Stephen !   O, the wayward boy,
   How I have wept and prayed for him !
I've waited for the answer long,
   And oftentimes my faith grew dim ;
But God has promised—He'll fulfil,
   Although His way may not be mine.
If I am gone before he comes—
   For, children, he will come some time—

Tell him that in the silent hours
  Of darksome night, when all alone,
I've made a ladder of my prayers,
  Reaching from earth to God's white throne.
When he finds that he feeds on husks,
  And longs for bread he can climb there.
God, for Christ's sake, will take him home ;
  Then he'll find bread enough to spare.

This is my legacy for him,
  But don't upbraid about the past ;
When he comes back, be sure and say
  That mother loved him to the last.
Father and I toiled hard to save
  Something each year to lay aside,
That you might all have legacies
  To help you on, if we both died.

But crops failed often, times were hard ;
  One year the drought destroyed the grain;
Another year was just as bad—
  We had such heavy falls of rain.
Then I would fret when things went wrong,
  But father always used to say,
Perhaps, if we could see the road,
  We'd find an angel in the way.

But father died ; you know the rest.
  You've done nobly and bravely, John ;
Your strength of arm and noble heart,
  For years, I have depended on.
Perhaps it's better as it is ;
  Wealth envy brings and foolish strife.
Wills oft are broken in the courts,
  And friends made enemies for life.

Of this world's goods we always had
    Only a small and meagre share ;
So I can leave to you and yours
    Only my blessing and my prayer.
The sun has set.   Upon your heads
    I'll place my hands.   God bless you all.
Give me your arm, John, I'll go in,
    The heavy dew begins to fall.

BROWN HANDS.

BY MRS. HATTIE F. BELL.

FULL many a page has been written,
    And the gifted have sung in the praise
Of lily white hands and fingers
    In a score of poetical ways ;
This is all very well for a lady
    Who lives among diamonds and silk,
But sometimes in life a farmer's wife
    Is obliged to do housework and milk.
And woman's best mission thro'out our dear land
Is fulfilled in the strength of the little brown hand.

When the roses are blushing the sweetest,
    And the vines climb up to the eaves,
And the robins are rocking their birdies
    To sleep 'mong the maple leaves ;
The sunshine smiles down 'cross the threshold,
    When the labour of love seems but rest,
Whether rocking the household birdies,
    Or keeping the dear home-nest—
Oh ! I pity you all who can't understand
The wealth and the worth of a little brown hand.

If I were a man with a fortune,
   A million laid by on the shelf—
If I were a youth—if I wasn't, in truth,
   If I wasn't a woman myself—
I know what I'd do in a minute,
   (White fingers have often misled) ;
I'd seek after those whose rich tinting shows
   Acquaintance with puddings and bread.
I'd use all the eloquence words could command,
And be proud might I win a little brown hand.

CALLED BY THE ANGELS.

THE farmer's wife is sitting alone,
   In the dusk of a winter's day,
While over the hills the shadows fall,
   And over the meadows grey,
And the cares of many a busy hour
   Steal fast from her heart away.

Her eyes have wandered through mist of tears
   To the churchyard under the hill,
Where the snow, like the wings of a brooding dove,
   Lies soft and pure and still,
And where her treasures, so long ago,
   She laid at the Master's will.

And ah ! how oft, as the days go by,
   She starts, as her listening ear
Has almost caught on the passing breeze
   Voices so sweet and clear.
" 'Tis the angels calling !" she thinks. " Ah me !
   It is weary waiting here."

The farmer comes from his work, at last,
　In the dusk of a winter's day,
And he sits him down by his faithful wife,
　And she parts his locks so gray,
And looks in his face with a loving smile
　That years steal never away.

And back again, as her dim eyes turn
　To the hills where the shadows fall,
She thinks, " My treasures are lying there.
　But He has not taken *all*,
Since one is waiting beside me still
　Till the angels' voices call."

But the weeks are slow, and the aged two,
　In the dusk of many a day,
Will watch the shadows come and go
　O'er the meadows cold and grey,
Ere they, at the Master's will, may lie
　Where their treasures are laid away.

GREAT NEWS.

　" We've got thome newth at our houth,
　　Ith funny and ith true,
　Ith made uth all tho happy,
　　'Twill make you happy too ! "

And pretty Kitty Allen
　Had such an eager look,
The tall, grave man before her,
　Laid down his pondrous book

He stroked her fair, bright ringlets,
  And took her on his knee,
And said, " Well, tell me Kitty,
  What this great news can be."

" You gueth ; I cannot tell you
  Right thraight off ; Kitty said,
And 'neath her tiny kerchief,
  She hid her roguish head.

" I guess you've found three kittens,
  With your old tortoise cat ; "
" No ; you've got to guess again ;
  Ith better newth than that ! "

" I guess your mamma's bought you
  A pretty little hat.".
" O, pho ! you thilly gentleman,
  Ith better newth than *that* ! "

" I give up, Kitty ; tell me ; "
  Her wise, rich neighbour said,
And then she drew her kerchief
  From off her flaxen head,

And said, " Then I will tell you.
  Its jutht ath true ath truth,—
Our own thweet, darlin' baby
  Hath got a little tooth ! "

Down from his knee she sprang, off
  In merry glee she ran ;
" I want to thee that toothie,
  Jutht as quick'th I can ! "

O happy, careless Kitty!
  This wise man's books and gold,
Are less to him, than is to thee
  The news so proudly told.

KATRINA.

You don't know who Katrina is?
  Why, she's our newest dolly;
She's sister to wax Eveline,
  First cousin to Miss Molly.
She only came to us last week,
  Afraid of every stranger;
And so we kept old pussy out,
  The Kittens, and black Ranger.

And yet we left a little foe,
  When we went out a-walking;
Our darling, silly baby dear,
  With mamma sweetly talking.
Mamma went up to get her work;
  Pet caught up dear Katrina,
And laid her on the register,
  O, dear! you should have seen her!

Mamma came back, but 'twas too late;
  Her cheeks were boiling over,
Her eyes were shedding waxen tears,
  Before mamma could move her!
All baby said was, " Poo' Katrine!
  She cold, and baby warm her;
And now she very sick; O, dear!
  Go get the me'cine, mamma!"

That was the end of sweet Katrine ;
  We still have Eve and Molly ;
And better yet the baby dear
  That warmed our waxen dolly.
With many tears we wrapped Katrine,
  And put her safe away,
To show Miss Mischief what she did
  On this sad Christmas Day.

I'M HURRIED, CHILD!

"O, MOTHER, look ! I've found a butterfly
Hanging upon a leaf—do tell me why there was
    no butter.
Oh, do see its wings ! I never saw such pretty
    things,
All streaked and striped with blue and brown
    and gold.
Where is its house when all the days are cold ?"
" Yes, yes," she said, in absent accents mild—
              " I'm hurried, child !"

" Last night my dolly quite forgot her prayers ;
An' when she thought you had gone down the
    stairs,
An' dolly was afraid ; an' so I said,
' Just don't you mind, but say them in the bed,
Because I think that God is just as near.'
When dolls are 'fraid do you 'spose He can hear ?"
The mother spoke from out the ruffles piled—
              " I'm hurried, child !"

"Oh, come and see the flowers in the sky
The sun has left, and *won't* you, by-and-by,
Dear mamma, take me in your arms and tell
Me all about the Pussy in the Well?
Then tell me of the babies in the wood?
An' then, perhaps, about Red Riding Hood?"
"Too much to do—hush, hush, you drive me
       wild.
              "I'm hurried, child!"

The little one grew very quiet now;
And grieved and puzzled was the childish brow;
And then it queried: "Mother do you know
The reason 'cause you must be hurried so?
I think the hours are little-er than I,
So I will take my pennies, and will buy
A bigger clock! O, big as it can be,
              For you and me!"

      *   *   *   *

The mother now has leisure infinite.
She sits with folded hands and face as white
As winter. In her heart is winter's chill.
She sits at leisure questioning of God's will—
"My child has ceased to breathe, and all is night.
Is heaven so dark that Thou didst grudge my light?
O life! O God! I must discover why
              Time moves so slowly by."

O, mothers sweet, if cares must ever fall,
Pray do not make them stones to build a wall
Between thee and thy own; and miss thy right
To blessedness, so swift to take its flight!

While answering baby questionings you are
But entertaining angels unawares.
The richest gifts are gathered by the way
For darkest day.

THE GIRL WITH THE CALICO DRESS.

A FIG for your upper-ten girls,
    With their velvets, and satins, and laces,
Their diamonds, and rubies, and pearls,
    And their milliner figures and faces ;
They may shine at a party or ball,
    Emblazoned with half they possess ;
But give me, in place of them all,
    My girl with the calico dress.

She is plump as a partridge, and fair
    As the rose in its earliest bloom ;
Her teeth will with ivory compare,
    And her breath with the clover perfume ;
Her step is as free and as light
    As the fawn's whom the hunters hard press,
And her eye is as soft and as bright—
    My girl with the calico dress.

She is cheerful, warm-hearted and true,
    And is kind to her father and mother ;
She studies how much she can do
    For her little sweet sister and brother ;
If you want a companion for life,
    To comfort, enliven and bless,
She is just the right sort of a wife—
    My girl with the calico dress.

DOT AND DOLLY.

BY MINNIE WARD PATTISON.

Sweet little Dot on the doorstep sits, with Dolly
    wrapped in a shawl—
Her own thin dress is faded and patched, but
    Dolly has none at all !
She kisses and cuddles her little pet in a way 'tis
    joy to see,
And whispers, " I know we's poor, but I's got
    you and *you's* got *me !*"

Rocking her treasure to and fro, in the silent
    summer air,
Her chubby chin to her bosom went, and her
    hands forgot their care,
Her dimpled feet into dreamland slipped, just as
    upon the scene
A lady rode, with jewels and silk begirt like a
    very queen.

Her happy darling, just Dot's own size, the child
    and the Dolly spied ;
She pointed, grasping her mamma's arm, to the
    half-wrapped pet and cried—
" Oh mamma ! look at her dolly—see ! arn't you
    'fraid it's catching cold ?
Please let me give it Rosa's dress—you know it's
    getting old."

She slipped from the carriage, and quick the
    work of the little maid was done,
And Dot's poor dolly was in a dress the
    prettiest under the sun !
Gold and silver, satin and gauze, stockings and
    bright blue shoes,
And money, as much in her pocket put as a doll
    in a year could use.

Then away, with a smile that almost laughed, so
    great was the giver's glee,
She went, with many a backward look, and said,
    " I's afraid she'll see !
Hurry up Tom—mamma !" and quick away to
    their palace home they flew,
While Dot was dreaming a wonderful dream
    of fairies and Dolly, too.

They had satin dresses, and gauzy wings, all
    speckled with drops of gold ;
They danced in troops on the lilac leaves, and a
    leaf would a dozen hold ;
And Dolly was dancing with all her might in
    the prettiest dress of all,
And spangled wings, when up sprang Dot, afraid
    lest her pet should fall.

She opened her eyes, and merrily laughed, in
    happiness and surprise,
As Dolly, dressed in her fairy best, looked into
    her wondering eyes.
" Oh mamma ! what shall I do ?" cried Dot, in a
    comic tone of dismay,
" My Dolly has borrowed a fairy's clothes, and
    the fairies have runned away !

O, the bright dreams in bye-lo-land !
All by the loving angels planned !
Soft little lashes downward close,
Just like the petals of a rose.
   Swing so,
   Bye-lo !
Prettiest eyes in Bye-lo-land.

Sweet is the way to Bye-lo-land,
Guided by mother's gentle hand ;
Little lambs now are in the fold,
Little birds nestle from the cold.
   Swing so,
   Bye-lo !
Baby is safe in Bye-lo-land.

———

LOVE'S SOVEREIGNTY.

BY JOHN G. SAXE.

Though Love loves well all things of outward grace
 That poets praise and gentle ladies prize,
 Yet lives he not by favour of blue eyes,
Or black or brown, or aught that he may trace
In features faultless as the perfect face
 Of Art's ideal. No! his essence lies
 Deep in the heart, not in its changing dyes
On lip and cheek. He has his dwelling-place
 In the life's life. As violets deck the May—
 Which yet survives when these have passed away,
All lovely things are Love's ; but, ne'ertheless,
 Health, youth, and beauty, though they serve
  him well,
 Are but Love's ministers ; his sovereign spell
Lives in his own immortal loveliness !

MAMMA'S SICK.

LITTLE brave boy at the gate,
  Run and play ; why do you wait ?
"Hush your noise, old carts, I say,
  My dear mamma's sick to-day !"

Little "Pink-boots" on the stair,
  Why so silent stand you there ?
In a whisper hear her say,
  "Hush ! my mamma's sick to-day."

Little maid with thoughtful eye,
  Softly singing "Lullaby,"
You are not the nurse alway ?.
  "No ; but mamma's sick to-day."

Happy mother ! she has heard
  Tiptoe step and whispered word ;
Love has almost cured her pain ;
  Soon she will be well again.

HER MOTHER'S EAR.

BY EMMA M. JOHNSON.

They sat at the spinning together,
  And they spun the fine white thread ;
One face was old and the other young,
  A golden and silver head.

And at times the young voice broke in song,
  That was wonderfully sweet,
And the mother's heart beat deep and calm,
  For her joy was most complete.

D

And at times the mother counselled,
    In a voice so soft and low,
How the untried feet of her daughter
    Through this strange, rough life should go.

There was many a holy lesson,
    Inwoven with silent prayer,
Taught to her gentle, listening child
    As they two sat spinning there.

" And of all that I speak, my darling,
    From my older head and heart,
God giveth me one last thing to say,
    And with it thou shalt not part :

" Thou wilt listen to many voices—
    And, ah woe, that this must be !—
The voice of praise and the voice of love
    And the voice of flattery ;

" But listen to me, my little one,
    There's one thing that thou shalt fear,
Let never a word to my love be said
    Which her mother may not hear.

" No matter how true, my darling one,
    The words may seem to thee,
They are not fit for my child to hear
    If they cannot be told to me.

" If thou wilt keep thy young heart pure,
    And thy mother's heart from fear,
Bring all that is told to thee by day
    At night to thy mother's ear."

And thus they sat spinning together,
  And an angel bent to see
The mother and child whose happy life
  Went on so lovingly.

And a record was made by his golden pen,
  And this on his page he said,
That the mother who counselled her child so well,
  Need never to feel afraid ;

For God would keep the heart of the child
  Who, with tender love and fear,
Should kneel at her mother's side at night,
  With lips to her mother's ear !

WAITING FOR THE CHILDREN.

BY AIMEE HOWARD.

GATH'RING flowers in the sunshine,
  With their petals bright with dew,
Merry little figures flitting ;
  Eyes of bonny brown and blue.
When the twilight shades are falling,
  Little feet have ceased to roam,
And the forms within the doorway
  Greet the children coming home.

Working in life's golden vineyard,
  When the sweets of youth are past,
Waiting 'till the sheaves have ripened,
  And the harvest come at last !
When the marriage bells are pealing,
  High within the sacred dome,
Still the forms, grown older, dearer,
  Wait the children coming home.

Time is fleet, and Age will touch us,
    As he hurries on his way ;
Tarries not to smile or flatter,
    Till the sunset of our day.
Ne'er again on earth will listen
    Those dear forms in evening's gloam ;
But above, methinks, they're waiting
    For the children coming home.

BEAUTIFUL GRANDMAMMA.

BY MARJORY WEST.

GRANDMAMMA sits in her quaint arm-chair,
Never was lady more sweet and fair;
Her grey locks ripple like silver shells,
And her placid brow its story tells
Of gentle life and peaceful even,
A trust in God and a hope in heaven.

Little girl May sits rocking away,
In her own low seat, like some winsome fay ;
Two doll babies her kisses share,
And another one lies by the side of her chair.
May is fair as the morning dew,
Cheeks of roses and ribbons of blue.

"Say, grandmamma," says the pretty elf,
"Tell me a story about yourself ;
When you were little, what did you play ?
Where you good or naughty the whole long day ?
Was it hundreds and hundreds of years ago ?
And what makes your soft hair as white as snow ?

" Did you have a mamma to hug and kiss ?
And a dolly like this, and this, and this ?
Did you have a pussy like my little Kate ?
Did you go to bed when the clock struck eight ?
Did you have long curls and beads like mine,
And a new silk apron and ribbons fine ? "

Grandmamma smiled at the little maid,
And, laying aside her knitting, she said :
" Go to my desk, and a red box you'll see ;
Carefully lift it, and bring it to me."
So May put her dollies away and ran,
Saying : " I'll be as careful as ever I can."

Then grandmamma opened the box, and lo !
A beautiful child with throat like snow,
Lips just tinted like pink shells rare,
Eyes of hazel, golden hair.
Hands all dimpled, and teeth like pearls—
Fairest and sweetest of little girls.

' O, who is it ? " cried winsome May.
" How I wish she were here to-day !
Wouldn't I love her like everything ?
Wouldn't I wish her frolic and sing !
Say, dear grandmamma, who can she be ? "
" Darling," said grandma, " that child was me."

May looked long at the dimpled grace,
And then at the saint-like, fair old face ;
" How funny ! " she cried, with a smile and a kiss,
To have such a dear little grandma as this !
" Still," she added, with smiling zest,
" I think, dear grandma, I like you best ! "

So May climbed on the silken knee,
And grandmamma told her history :
What plays she played, what toys she had,
How at times she was naughty, or good, or sad ;
" But the best thing you did," said May, " don't
      you see,
Was to grow a beautiful grandma for me."

THE ANGEL'S LADDER.

BY MRS. M. B. BUTTS.

" If there were a ladder, mother,
    Between the earth and sky,
As in the days of the Bible,
    I would bid you all good-bye,
And go through every country,
    And search from town to town,
Till I had found the ladder,
    With angels coming down.

" Then I would wait, quite softly,
    Beside the lowest round,
Till the sweetest-looking angel
    Had stepped upon the ground ;
I would pull his dazzling garment,
    And speak out very plain :
' Will you take me, please, to heaven,
    When you go back again ?' "

" Ah, darling," said the mother,
    " You need not wonder so
To find the golden ladder
    Where angels come and go.

"Wherever gentle kindness,
　Or pitying love, abounds,
There is the wondrous ladder
　With angels on the rounds."

MY NEIGHBOUR'S BABY.

ACROSS in my neighbour's window,
　With its drapings of satin and lace,
I see, 'neath its flowing ringlets,
　A baby's innocent face.
His feet in crimson slippers,
　Are tapping the polished glass,
And the crowd in the streets look upward
　And nod and smile as they pass.

Just here in my cottage window,
　Catching flies in the sun,
With a patched and faded apron,
　Stands my own little one.
His face is as pure and handsome
　As the baby's over the way,
And he keeps my heart from breaking
　At my toiling, every day.

Sometimes when the day is ended,
　And I sit in the dusk to rest,
With the face of my sleeping darling
　Hugged close to my lonely breast,
I pray that my neighbour's baby
　May not catch heaven's roses all,
But that some may crown the forehead
　Of my loved one, as they fall.

And when I draw the stockings
  From his little weary feet,
And kiss the rosy dimples
  In his limbs so round and sweet,
I think of the dainty garments
  Some little children wear,
And that my God withholds them
  From mine so pure and fair.

     *   *   *   *

May God forgive my envy—
  I knew not what I said ;
My heart is crushed and troubled,
  My neighbour's boy is dead !
I saw the little coffin
  As they carried it out to-day ;—
A mother's heart is breaking
  In the mansion over the way.

The light is fair in my window ;
  The flowers bloom at my door ;
My boy is chasing the sunbeams
  That dance on the cottage floor.
The roses of health are blooming
  On my darling's cheek to-day,
But the baby has gone from the window
  Of the mansion over the way.

LITTLE CHILDREN.

THERE is music, there is sunshine,
  Where the little children dwell,
In the cottage, in the mansion,
  In the hut or in the cell ;

There is music in their voices,
　There is sunshine in their love,
And a joy for ever round them,
　Like a glory from above.

Little children ! yes, we love them
　For their spirit's ceaseless flow,
For the joy that ever lingers
　Where their bounding footsteps go ;
'Tis the sunshine of their presence
　Makes the lowly cottage fair,
And the palace is a prison
　If no little one is there.

Oh ! I wonder not the Saviour,
　He, the beautiful, the meek,
To the precious little children,
　Tender, loving words did speak.
'Tis a pleasant thing to teach them
　Unto Him to bend the knee,
Since He spoke the words of blessing,
　" Suffer them to come to Me."

Yea, of such is heaven's kingdom,
　And if we would enter there,
We must seek the sinless garment
　Which the little child doth wear.
Father, bless the little children,
　Bless them everywhere they dwell—
In the palace, in the mansion,
　In the hut, or in the cell ;
May the clouds of sin and sorrow
　Never darken o'er their way,
And in heart may we be like them,
　Pure and innocent as they.

MAMMA'S KISSES.

BY A. E. FABENS.

A KISS when I wake in the morning,
  A kiss when I go to bed,
A kiss when I burn my finger,
  A kiss when I bump my head.

A kiss when my bath is over,
  A kiss when my bath begins ;
My mamma is full of kisses,
  As full as nurse is of pins.

A kiss when I play with my rattle,
  A kiss when I pull her hair ;
She covered me over with kisses
  The day I fell from the stair.

A kiss when I gave her trouble,
  A kiss when I gave her joy ;
There's nothing like mamma's kisses
  For her own little baby boy.

THE WOMAN.

JAMES RUSSELL LOWELL.

NOT as all other women are
  Is she that to my soul is dear ;
Her glorious fancies come from far,
Beneath the silver evening star ;
  And yet her heart is ever near.

Great feelings hath she of her own,
  Which lesser souls may never know ;
God giveth them to her alone,
And sweet they are as any tone
  Wherewith the wind may choose to blow.

Yet in herself she dwelleth not,
  Although no home were half so fair ;
No simplest duty is forgot ;
Life hath no dim and lowly spot
  That doth not in her sunshine share.

She doeth little kindnesses,
  Which most leave undone or despise;
For nought that sets one heart at ease,
And giveth happiness or peace,
  Is low esteemed in her eyes.

She hath no scorn of common things ;
  And though she seem of other birth,
Round us her heart entwines and clings,
And patiently she folds her wings
  To tread the humble paths of earth.

Blessing she is ; God made her so ;
  And deeds of week-day holiness
Fall from her noiseless as the snow ;
Nor hath she ever chance to know
  That aught were easier than to bless.

She is most fair, and thereunto
  Her life doth rightly harmonise ;
Feeling or thought that was not true
Ne'er made less beautiful the blue
  Unclouded heaven of her eyes.

She is a woman—one in whom
    The spring-time of her childish years
Hath never lost its fresh perfume,
Though knowing well that life hath room
    For many blights and many tears.

I love her with a love as still
    As a broad river's peaceful might,
Which by high tower and lowly mill,
Goes wandering at its own sweet will,
    And yet doth ever flow aright.

And on its full, deep breast serene,
    Like quiet isles my duties lie ;
It flows around them and between,
And makes them fresh, and fair, and green—
    Sweet homes wherein to live and die.

———

HELPING PAPA AND MAMMA.

PLANTING the corn and potatoes,
    Helping to scatter the seeds,
Feeding the hens and the chickens,
    Freeing the garden from weeds,
Driving the cows to the pasture,
    Feeding the horse in the stall—
We little children are busy ;
    Sure there is work for us all,
        Helping papa.

Spreading the hay in the sunshine,
    Raking it up when 't is dry,
Picking the apples and peaches
    Down in the orchard hard by,

Picking the grapes in the vineyard,
   Gathering nuts in the fall—
We little children are busy ;
   Yes, there is work for us all,
      Helping papa.

Sweeping and washing the dishes,
   Bringing the wood from the shed,
Ironing, sewing, and knitting,
   Helping to make up the bed,
Taking good care of the baby,
   Watching her lest she should fall—
We little children are busy ;
   O, there is work for us all,
      Helping mamma.

Work makes us cheerful and happy,
   Makes us both active and strong ;
Play we enjoy all the better
   When we have laboured so long.
Gladly we help our kind parents,
   Quickly we come at their call ;
Children should love to be busy ;
   There is much work for us all,
      Helping papa and mamma.

GROWING OLD.

SOFTLY, O, softly the years have swept by thee,
   Touching thee lightly with tenderest care ;
Sorrow and death they did often bring nigh thee,
   Yet they have left thee but beauty to wear.
      Growing old gracefully,
      Gracefully fair.

Far from the storms that are lashing the ocean,
  Nearer each day to the pleasant home-light ;
Far from the waves that are big with commotion,
  Under full sail, and the harbour in sight.
        Growing old cheerfully,
        Cheerful and bright.

Past all the winds that are adverse and chilling,
  Past all the islands that lured thee to rest,
Past all the currents that wooed thee unwilling
  Far from the port and the land of the blest.
        Growing old peacefully,
        Peaceful and blest.

Never a feeling of envy or sorrow
  When the bright faces of children are seen ;
Never a year from their youth wouldst thou
    borrow ;   .
  Thou dost remember what lieth between.
        Growing old willingly,
        Gladly, I ween.

Eyes that grow dim to the earth and its glory
  See but the brighter the heavenly glow !
Ears that are full to the world and its story
  Drink in the songs that from Paradise flow ;
        All their sweet recompense
        You cannot know.

Fourscore !   But softly the years have swept by
    thee,
  Touching thee lightly with tenderest care ;
Sorrow and death they did often bring nigh thee,
  Yet they have left thee but beauty to wear ;
        Growing old gracefully,
        Graceful and fair.

"IF I SHOULD DIE TO-NIGHT."

IF I should die to-night,
My friends would look upon my quiet face,
Before they laid it in its resting-place,
And deem that death had left it almost fair ;
And laying snow-white flowers against my hair,
Would smooth it down with tearful tenderness,
And fold my hands, with lingering caress—
Poor hands, so empty and so cold to-night.

If I should die to-night,
My friends would call to mind, with loving
    thought,
Some kindly deed the icy hand had wrought;
Some gentle word the frozen lips had said ;
Errands on which the willing feet had sped—
The memory of my selfishness and pride,
My hasty words, would all be put aside,
And so I should be loved and mourned to-night.

If I should die to-night,
Even hearts estranged would turn once more to
    me,
Recalling other days remorsefully.
The eyes that chill me with averted glance
Would look upon me as of yore, perchance,
And soften in the old familiar way—
For who would war with dumb, unconscious
    clay ?
So I might rest forgiven of all to-night.

O friends, I pray to-night,
Keep not your kisses for my dead, cold brow.
The way is lonely ; let me feel them now.
Think gently of me ; I am travel-worn ;
My faltering feet are pierced with many a thorn.
Forgive, O hearts estranged ! forgive, I plead !
When dreamless rest is mine, I shall not need
The tenderness for which I long to-night.

LEFT ALONE AT EIGHTY.

WHAT did you say, dear—breakfast ?
    Somehow I've slept too late ;
You are very kind, dear Effie ;
    Go tell them not to wait.
I'll dress as quick as ever I can,
    My old hands tremble sore,
And Polly, who used to help, dear heart !
    Lies t'other side o' the door.

Put up the old pipe, deary,
    I couldn't smoke to-day ;
I'm sort o' dazed and frightened,
    And don't know what to say.
It's lonesome in the house, here,
    And lonesome out o' door—
I never knew what lonesome meant,
    In all my life before.

The bees go humming, the whole day long,
    And the first June rose has blown,
And I am eighty, dear Lord, to-day,—
    Too old to be left alone !

O, heart of love ! so still and cold,
   O, precious lips, so white !—
For the first sad hours in sixty years,
   You were out of my reach last night.

You've cut the flower. You're very kind.
   She rooted it last May ;
It was only a slip ; I pulled the rose,
   And threw the stem away ;
But she, sweet, thrifty soul, bent down,
   And planted it where she stood,
" Dear, maybe the flowers are living," she said,
   " Asleep, in this bit of wood."

I can't rest, deary—I cannot rest ;
   Let the old man have his will,
And wander from porch to garden post—
   The house is so deathly still ;
Wander, and long for a sight of the gate
   She has left ajar for me—
We had got so used to each other, dear,
   So used to each other, you see.

Sixty years, and so wise and good,
   She made me a better man
From the moment I kissed her fair young face,
   And our lovers' life began.
And seven fine boys she has given me,
   And out of the seven, not one
But the noblest father in all the land
   Would be proud to call his son.

O, well, dear Lord, I'll be patient,
   But I feel so broken up ;
At eighty years it's an awsome thing
   To drain such a bitter cup.

                      E

I know there's Joseph, and John, and Hal,
    And four good men beside,
But a hundred sons couldn't be to me
    Like the woman I made my bride.

My little Polly, so bright and fair ;
    So winsome, and good, and sweet !
She had roses twined in her sunny hair,
    White shoes on her dainty feet ;
And I held her hand—was it yesterday
    That we stood up to be wed ?
And—No, I remember, I'm eighty to-day,
    And my dear wife, Polly, is dead.

OUR AVIS.

BY REV. JAMES UPHAM, D.D.

SHE loved the tiny flowers
    Just peering from the sod,
Or decking door and bowers—
    Those cheery smiles of God.

And yet she was an infant
    Within her mother's arms—
The sweetest of the smiles of God,
    The crown of earthly charms.

She came while autumn lingered ;
    The chill months quickly passed ;
Earth decked itself with beauty—
    It was her first and last.

The morning glory loved so well,
　Type fit of her brief stay,
Now types the glory of the morn
　Of her eternal day.

———

" As tender mothers guiding baby steps,
When places come at which the tiny feet
Would trip, lift up the little ones in arms
Of love, and set them down beyond the harm ;
So did our Father watch the precious child
Led o'er the stones by me, who stumbled oft
Myself, but strove to help my darling on ;
He saw the sweet limbs faltering, and saw
Rough ways before us, where my arms would fail,
So reached from heaven, and lifting the dear
　　child,
Who smiled in leaving me, He put her down
Beyond all hurt, beyond my sight, and bade
Her wait for me !　Shall I not then be glad,
And thanking God press on to overtake ?"

———

ONE OF GOD'S POOR.

BY MYRA COPELAND.

She died all alone at dead of night,
　No neighbour nor friend was near,
To wipe the cold sweat from her furrowed brow,
　Or whisper one word of cheer ;
No loving hand to close the sad eyes,
　So sunken by grief and pain,
To fold the worn hands a-weary of toil,
　Never to weary again.

"She died very poor," the neighbours said,
    As they stood in the cheerless room,
So dreary and dark, so damp and cold,
    So full of shadows and gloom.
"Poor thing," they said, "we have come too late—
    Too late to do any good."
And they saw with pain the lack of fire,
    The lack of clothing and food.

But better we knew who knew her life,
    So patient, faithful, and true ;
So strong and brave, God's will her delight,
    Her joy his bidding to do.
A patience well-kept through bitter pain,
    A faith that no trial could dim,
And strength to follow God's leading hand,
    Content to be led by Him.

She died very rich. Heir to a crown,
    A throne, and a wondrous estate ;
A name that shall stand above the names
    Of all the wise and the great.
Close the dim eyes and fold the thin hands,
    While angels exultingly sing,
"She died very rich, a child of God !
    Joint heir with the Son of a King !"

MY CHOICE.

BY JENNIE HARRISON.

Yes, I know there are stains on my carpet —
    The traces of small, muddy boots ;
And I see your fair tapestry glowing
    All spotless with blossoms and fruits.

And I know that my walls are disfigured
　With prints of small fingers and hands ;
And I see that your own household whiteness
　All fresh in its purity stands.

Yes, I know my " black walnut" is battered,
　And dented by many small heels, ;
While your own polished stairway, all perfect,
　Its smooth shining surface reveals.

And I know that my parlour is littered
　With many odd treasures and toys ;
While your own is in daintiest order,
　Unharmed by the presence of boys.

And I know that my room is invaded
　Quite boldly, all hours of the day ;
While you sit in your own unmolested,
　And dream the soft quiet away.

Yes, I know I have jackets that wear out,
　And buttons that never will stay ;
While you can embroider at leisure,
　And learn pretty arts of " croquet."

And I know there are lessons of spelling,
　Which I must be patient to hear ;
While you may sit down to your novel,
　Or turn the last magazine near.

Yes, I know there are four little bedsides,
　Where I must stand watchful, each night ;
While you may go out in your carriage,
　And flash in your dresses so bright.

Now I think I'm a neat little woman—
   I like my house orderly, too ;
And I'm fond of all dainty belongings—
   Yet I would not change places with you.

No ! keep you fair home, with its order,
   Its freedom from trouble and noise ;
And keep your own fanciful leisure—
   But give me my four splendid boys.

ALWAYS REJOICING.

"REJOICE ALWAYS ; REJOICE, I SAY, IN
THE LORD."

Ah ! don't be sorrowful, darling,
   And don't be sorrowful, pray :
Taking the year together, my dear,
   There isn't more night than day.

'Tis rainy weather, my darling,
   Time's waves they heavily run ;
But taking the year together, my dear,
   There isn't more cloud than sun.

We are old folks now, my darling,
   Our heads are growing grey ;
And taking the year to-gether, my dear,
   You will always find the May.

We have had our May, my darling,
   And our roses, long ago ;
And the time of the year is coming, my dear
   For the silent night and snow.

And God is God, my darling,
   Of night as well as day,
And we feel and know that we can go
   Wherever He leads the way.

Ay, God of the night, my darling,
   Of the night of death so grim ;
The gate that leads out of life, good wife,
   Is the gate that leads to Him.

LITTLE ROMP.

I'M tired to death of keeping still,
   And being good all day ;
I guess my mamma's company
   Forgot to go away,
I've wished and wished they'd think of it,
   And mamma's wished so too,
But they must talk forever first,
   They almost always do !

I heard Tom calling me once,
   He's launched his boat, I know,
I wanted to go out and help—
   But mamma's eyes said no.
The ladies talk such stuff to me,
   It makes me sick to hear—
" How beautiful your hair curls ! " or
   " How red your cheeks are, dear ! "

I'd ten times rather run a race
   Than play my tunes and things ;
I wouldn't swap my dogs and balls
   For forty diamond rings.

I've got no 'finement, aunty says,
　　I 'spect she knows the best ;
I don't need much to climb a tree
　　Or hunt a squirrel's nest.

" Girls are like berries," papa says,
　　" Sweeter for running wild."
But Aunt Melissa shakes her head,
　　And calls me " horrid child."
I'll always be a romp, she knows—
　　But sure's my name is Sadie,
I'll fool 'em all some dreadful day
　　By growing up a lady.

WILL'S WIDOW.

BY ISABELLA FYVIE MAYO.

It may seem hard to work so long,
　　And get such little pay ;
But still it does not matter much,
　　As Will has gone away ;
That shows you ma'am, how true it is God's ways
　　are always best :
He takes the good we miss the most, and we
　　don't miss the rest !

A cup of tea and bite of bread
　　Are quite enough for me ;
I wouldn't wish another thing,
　　As Will's not here to see ;
Or, leastways, if he can look down, he knows too
　　much to care,
Knows that it does not matter much what
　　people eat or wear.

If I was living in the place
　　Where I once lived with Will,
Just going on the some old way,
　　But with the house grown still,
I think Will would seem farther off—the days
　　would pass so slow.
One needn't sit to watch for Death—he's sure to
　　come, we know.

But now I seldom moan and pine
　　About the sadder part.
I think the moving of the hands
　　Is wholesome for the heart ;
For as I work I recollect the happy life we had—
Our courting time, and wedding day, when all
　　the earth seemed glad.

That is Will's linnet overhead,
　　I think it pines for trees,
So whiles when Sunday evening comes
　　I take it for a breeze ;
Will's lying not so far from this, and that is where
　　we go ;
The little bird it cheeps and cheeps —what
　　mayn't such creatures know ?

Will's buried by an old grey church
　　That stands upon a hill,
And as I can't take Dick inside,
　　I listen at the sill ;
And every word the parson speaks, I seem to hear
　　Will say,
" That's something good for you, old girl," for
　　that was poor Will's way.

And all the way as I walk home
 I watch the sun go down ;
It makes the grim old city look
 Like new Jerusalem town ;
And I have such sweet fancies come I never had
  before ;
When you've none else to talk with you, I think
 God talks the more.

When first Will went, I longed to die,
 But now I wait content,
As parson says, " When comforts go
 The Comforter is sent."
Yet I'll be glad to meet with Will, and tell him it
  came true,
When he said, " Polly, dear old girl, God will
 look after you."

———

SHE ALWAYS MADE HOME HAPPY.

In an old churchyard stood a stone,
 Weather-marked and stained ;
The hand of time had crumbled it,
 So only part of it remained ;
Upon one side could I just trace—
 " In memory of my mother ;"
An epitaph which spoke of " home "
 Was chiselled on the other.

I'd gazed on monuments of fame,
 High towering to the skies ;
I'd seen the sculptured marble stone
 Where a great hero lies ;

But by this epitaph I paused,
   And read it o'er and o'er,
For I had never seen inscribed
   Such words as these before.

" She always made home happy,"
   A noble record left,
A legacy of memory sweet
   To those she loved bereft ;
And what a testimony given
   By those who knew her best,
Engraven on this plain, rude stone,
   That marked the mother's rest !

It was a humble resting-place,
   I knew that they were poor,
But they had seen their mother sink
   And patiently endure.
They had marked her cheerful spirit
   When bearing, one by one,
Her many burdens up the hill,
   Till all her work was done.

So, when was stilled her weary heart,
   Folded her hands so white,
And she was carried from the home
   She'd always made so bright,
Her children made a monument
   That money can't secure,
As witness of a noble life,
   Whose record will endure.

A noble life ! but written not
   In any book of fame ;
Among the list of noted ones
   None ever saw her name ;

For only her own houschold knew
The victories she had won,
And none but they could testify
How well her work was done.

THE CROW THAT THE CROW CROWED.

BY S. CONANT FOSTER.

"Ho! ho!"
Said the crow:
"So I'm s'posed not to know
Where the rye and the wheat
And the corn kernels grow—
Ho! no!
Ho! ho!

"He! he!
Farmer Lee,
When I fly from my tree,
Just you see where the tops
Of the corn-ears will be;
Watch me!
He! he!

Switch-swirch,
With a lurch,
Flopped the bird from his perch,
As he spread out his wings
And set forth on his search—
His search,
Switch-swirch.

Click !—bang !—
How it rang,
How the small bullet sang
As it sped through the air—
And the crow, with a pang,
Went spang !—
Chi-bang !

THE TAIL FEATHERS.

Now know
That to crow
Often brings one to woe ;
Which the lines up above
Have been put there to show
And so
Don't crow.

ONLY A DOLL.

BY SARAH O. JEWETT.

Polly, my dolly ! why don't you grow ?
Are you a dwarf, my Polly ?
I'm taller and taller every day ;
How high the grass is !—do you see that ?
The flowers are growing like weeds, they say ?
The kitten is growing into a cat !
Why don't you grow, my dolly ?

Here is a mark upon the wall.
Look for yourself, my Polly !
I made it a year ago, I think.
I've measured you very often, dear,
But, though you've plenty to eat and drink,
You haven't grown a bit for a year.
Why don't you grow, my dolly ?

Are you never going to try to talk?
    You're such a silent Polly!
Are you never going to say a word?
    It isn't hard; and oh! don't you see
The parrot is only a little bird,
    But he can chatter so easily.
        You're quite a dunce, my dolly!

Let's go and play by the baby house;
    You are my dearest Polly!
There are other things that do not grow;
    Kittens can't talk, and why should you?
You are the prettiest doll, I know;
    You are a darling—that is true!
        Just as you are, my dolly!

I KNOW A BEAUTIFUL WOMAN.

BY MRS. FRANCIS D. GAGE.

I KNOW a beautiful woman,
    But she's not of "sweet sixteen";
Full sixty winters have come and gone
    The "Now" and "Then" between.
Yes, every year hath added
    A something so fair and true,
That to me she's the sweetest woman
    I think that ever I knew.

Her eye may be dimmer growing,
    It hath lost the glance of youth,
But up from the inner fountains
    It is flashing love and truth;

Her checks have not all the freshness
   Of the rosebud's glowing red ;
The purity of the lily,
   Full-blown, has come in its stead.

And her voice is low and soothing
   As the hum of summer bees,
Or twilight rustling 'mong the corn,
   Or the song of autumn trees.
She moves with a grace so gentle
   Among the garden bowers,
A brighter radiance than their own
   Seems falling on her flowers.

All over her face of beauty
   There are lines of days gone by—
Of holy loves and earnest hopes
   That have wrought there patiently ;
They are lovelier far than dimples,
   For I know that each was given
To mark the years of dutiful life
   That have fitted her for heaven.

I never think of that woman
   But my heart throbs high with love,
And I ask, " Can she be more beauteous
   In the blissful realms above ? "
I can scarcely in my dreaming
   See her face more fair and bright,
She seems to me now, with her radiant brow,
   A spirit of love and light.

The poet may sing his praises
   Of the glow of " sweet sixteen,"
But there's a holier beauty,
   Of sixty-five, I ween ;

For a girlish face that's moulded
  By a true and loving heart,
Will brighten as the heart throbs on,
  Rechiselling every part.

NAMING THE BABY.

BY MRS. RUFUS BARTLETT.

WHAT shall we call our baby
  Who lately to us came?
He's three months old to-day, and yet
  The darling has no name.
He now begins to smile and coo,
  And grasp at pretty things,
And acts as if he'd like to use
  A pair of tiny wings.

And as his tender mind expands
  Within his frame so small,
The music strain of baby's name
  Upon his ear should fall.
Let's call him "Winthrop"; that's a good
  Staunch Massachusetts name,
On which the pious Puritan
  Ne'er left a single stain.

Yet we must add another one;
  The mother now desires
Her cherub boy should bear the name—
  One that she loves—his sire's!
Now, baby, open wide your ears;
  You've oped your eyes so bright;
Winthrop Vanleuven,
  Keep the name forever pure and bright.

And now we to our little son
  An earthly name have given,
We'll consecrate his future life
  To usefulness and heaven.
Knowing this fair and fragile thing,
  All baby smiles and tears,
Contains a soul that will live on
  Through the immortal years.

O Thou who sent into our home
  This precious human flower,
Round which our yearning hearts now cling
  With such mysterious power,
Help us to write upon his heart,
  In childhood and in youth,
With burnished gold, the law of love,
  And royalty of truth.

Help us to guide his untried feet,
  So he at length shall stand,
With manhood's wreath upon his brow,
  A noble, Christian man.
And when his mission here shall close,
  And lowly sinks his frame,
O, 'mid the shining ones above
  Give him an angel's name.

THE LITTLE CHICKEN.

BY MRS. CHILION B. ALLEN.

I am a little chicken, hear me peep, peep, peep,
My mamma's gone away, and I've no place to
        sleep;
I feel a little lonely, but I will not say a word,

F

I don't like to be a chicken, I wish I were a bird.
I think I sing quite nicely, hear me peep, peep,
    peep,
Or weet, a weet a weet weet, cheap, cheap, cheap,
Now isn't that the nicest song you ever, ever
    heard ?
It is really very easy to be a little bird.

Now, when other little chicks are scratching in
    the dirt,
Or running to their mamma for fear they will
    be hurt,
I'll be singing far away, not so far I can't be
    heard,
For I want them all to know I'm no chicken ; I'm
    a bird.

What is that up in the heavens?   It's a hawk I
    really fear ?
If I could but find my mamma, how glad I'd be
    to see her.
"Cluck a cluck," that's mamma calling, sweeter
    sound I never heard ;
I'm so glad I am a chicken—I don't want to be
    a bird.

TOO LITTLE, EH ?

BY MARY MAPES DODGE.

Two little girls are better than one,
Two little boys can double the fun,
Two little birds can build a fine nest;
Two little arms can love mother best,

Two little ponies must go to a span,
Two little pockets has my little man,
Two little eyes to open and close,
Two little ears and one little nose,
Two little elbows, dimpled and sweet,
Two little shoes on two little feet,
Two little lips and one little chin,
Two little cheeks with a rose set in,
Two little shoulders chubby and strong,
Two little legs running all day long,
Two little prayers does my darling say,
Twice does he kneel by my side each day,
Two little folded hands, soft and brown,
Two little eyelids cast meekly down,
And two little angels guard him in bed,
One at the foot and one at the head.

THE LOST DOLL.

BY SARAH O. JEWETT.

THE sunflowers hang their heavy heads
   And wish the sun would shine ;
The clouds are gray, the wind is cold.
   " Where is that doll of mine ?
The dark is coming fast," said she.
   " I'm in a dreadful fright.
I don't know where I left my doll,
   And she'll be out all night.

" Twice up and down the garden walks
   I've looked ; but she's not there.
Oh ! yes, I've hunted in the hay ;
   I've hunted everywhere.

I must have left her out of doors ;
  But she is not in sight.
No Dolly in the summer-house,
  And she'll be out all night.

" The dew will wet her through and through
  And spoil her dear best dress ;
And she will wonder where I am
  And be in such distress ;
The dogs may find her in the grass,
  And bark and even bite ;
And all the bats will frighten her
  That fly about at night.

" I've not been down into the woods
  Or by the brook to-day.
I'm sure I had her in my arms
  When I came out to play,
Just after dinner ; then, I know,
  I watched Tom make his kite.
Will anybody steal my doll
  If she stays out all night ?

" I wonder where Papa has gone ?
  Why, here he comes ; and see !
He's bringing something in his hand.
  That's Dolly, certainly !
And so you found her in the chaise,
  And brought her home all right ?
I'll take her to the baby-house.
  I'm glad she's home to-night."

BUSY HANDS AND FEET.

LITTLE white hands have never
  Known what it is to work,

Yet they are busy ever,
   With never a wish to shirk.

Never a moment idle,
   Never at all o'ertasked ;
Whatever mamma calls for,
   Bringing as soon as asked.

Bringing the slippers for papa,
   And with them an evening kiss ;
Waiting to have his blessing
   Fill her with happiness,

Placing a chair for mamma,
   Without being asked at all ;
Soothing the fretting baby,
   Shaking her rattle small.

Playing when papa's reading,
   Still as a little mouse ;
Never with clash and clatter
   Righting her little house.

Never intrusive, only
   Ready to come and go
As papa or mamma wishes,
   Little face all aglow.

You may talk of your household jewels,
   But ours is the richest yet ;
O, what a priceless treasure
   We have in our little pet !

Ready at every one's bidding,
   With fingers so nimble and neat ;
Never such dutiful servants
   As these little hands and feet.

JOHNNY'S SOLILOQUY.

BY ANNIE A. PRESTON.

It seems to be father's greatest joy
To tell what he did when he was a boy.
Nothing very wonderful, so far's I can see ;
And it seems pretty rough on a fellow like me,
When I've worked like a man all the long sum-
      mer day—
And boys can get tired, I don't care what they
      say—
To have father declare, in his evening chat,
" When I was a boy I did better than that.

" I was bound out when I was boy,
Had never a play-day, a book, or a toy.
I earned my first suit when I was of age,
By working at odd hours for old Deacon Gage.
I often went barefoot, having seldom a hat,
And as for a coat, I was too poor for that.
Of course I had extra clothes in cold weather,
But the clothes were not broadcloth,
Nor the boots patent leather."

Then he talks of this and that wonderful feat,
With little to wear and little to eat ;
How he never went either to college or school,
Just picked up his learning without guide or rule,
And says : " John, to be sure, is easy to learn,
And always stands first at the close of the term ;
But if I'd his chance of books in *my* day,
I don't think you'd have found *me* always at play."

Now I am just as willing as can be to work,
Nobody can call me a bit of a shirk ;
I don't ask for fine clothes or frequent play-days,
For I know father's money has plenty of ways ;
But when I have done as well as I can,
They might treat me as though I'd some day be
      a man.
I'm so tired of the song father always has sung,
" I did better than that when I was young."

RELIGIOUS.

MOUNTING UP.

I COUNT this thing to be grandly true,
　That a noble deed is a step toward God,
　Lifting the soul from the common sod
To a purer air and a broader view.

We rise by things that are under our feet,
　By what we have mastered of good and gain:
　By the pride deposed and the passion slain,
And the vanquished hills that we hourly meet.

Heaven is not reached at a single bound;
　But we build the ladder by which we rise
　From the lowly earth to the vaulted skies;
And we mount to its summit round by round.

IS YOUR LAMP BURNING?

SAY, is your lamp burning, my brother?
　I pray you look quickly and see;
For if it were burning, then surely
　Some beams would fall bright upon me.

Straight, straight is the road, but I falter,
    And oft I fall out by the way ;
Then lift your lamp higher, my brother,
    Lest I should make fatal delay.

There are many and many around you
    Who follow wherever you go ;
If you thought that they walked in the shadow
    Your lamp would burn brighter, I know.

Upon the dark mountains they stumble,
    They are bruised on the rocks, and they lie
With their white, pleading faces turned upward
    To the clouds and the pitiful sky.

There is many a lamp that is lighted,
    We behold them anear and afar ;
But not many among them, my brother,
    Shine steadily on like a star.

I think, were they trimmed night and morning,
    They would never burn down or go out,
Though from the four quarters of Heaven
    The winds were all blowing about.

If once all the lamps that are lighted
    Would steadily blaze in a line,
Wide over the land and the ocean,
    What a girdle of glory would shine !

How all the dark places would brighten !
    How the mists would roll up and away !
How the earth would laugh out in her gladness
    To hail the millennial day !

Say, is your lamp burning, my brother?
  I pray you look quickly and see;
For if it were burning, then surely
  Some beams would fall bright upon me.

———

"COME."

BY MRS. L. S. HARRIS.

ONCE a ship's crew, worn and weary,
  Tossed on Galilee's dark waves,
Watched the mountain billows rising,
  Threatening but unfathomed graves;
And they saw no arm of succour
  Lent to still their hearts' wild cry,
Till a form, like spirit gliding,
  Whispered, " Fear not; it is I."

Thus it is, as o'er life's billows,
  'Mid the gloom of sorrow's night,
That same form is ever near us,
  Though obscured from natural sight.
Faith alone can hail His presence
  Through the mental sky's deep gloom;
Faith alone amid the breakers
  Hears that cheering voice say " Come."

" Come "—why longer toil in rowing?
  Walk with Him upon the wave;
All thy toil without His mercy
  Cannot thy frail life-barque save.
Heed not though the winds are raging,
  And the towering billows loom;
Keep the eye but fixed on Jesus;
  'Tis His voice that bids thee " Come."

Christian stranger, worn and weary,
  Toiling on life's boisterous deep,
Faint from labour unavailing,
  Sowing but where others reap,
Leave the ship with earth's frail tackling,
  Though to sense all's fraught with gloom ;
He can still thy grief's wild tempest,
  And His voice now bids thee "Come."

"JUST SIXTY-TWO."

JUST sixty-two ! Then trim thy light,
  And get thy jewels all re-set ;
'Tis past meridian, but bright,
  And lacks one hour to sunset yet.
      At sixty-two
      Be strong and true ;
Clear off thy rust, and shine anew.

'Tis yet high time ; thy staff resume,
  And fight fresh battles for the Truth ;
For what is age but youth's full bloom ;
  A riper, more transcendent youth ?
      A wedge of gold
      Is never old.
Streams broader grow as downward rolled.

At sixty-two life is begun ;
  At seventy-three begins once more !
Fly swifter as you near the sun,
  And brighter shine at eighty-four ;
      At ninety-five,
      Shouldst thou arrive,
Still wait on God, and work and thrive.

Keep thy locks wet with morning dew,
   And freely let thy graces flow ;
For life well spent is ever new,
   And years anointed younger grow.
        So work anew :
          Be young for aye ;
From sunset breaking into day.

THE OPEN CASEMENT AT BABYLON.

DANIEL vi. 10.

FROM THE GERMAN OF KARL GEROK.

BY REV. HENRY S. BURRAGE.

By the waters gently flowing
   Babylon's fair banks along,
Where the breezes, softly blowing,
   Move the leafy trees among,
In a chamber, by a casement,
   Which towards Zion open stands,
Daniel kneels in deep abasement,
   Seeking God with outstretched hands.

Daily thrice in rapt devotion
   Kneels he there before his Lord ;
Hushes the wild world's commotion,
   Claims the promise of the Word ;—
Morning, as the stars are fading,
   Midday, hour of fiercest heat,
Evening, in the twilight shading
   Busy Babel's lordly seat.

Palaces of monarchs spurning,
   Halls his exiled feet have trod,

Lo, the prophet, westward turning,
  Greets the Zion of his God.
And in gardens bright with flowers,
  Over many a palm-tree's crest,
Rise again the ruined towers
  Of Jerusalem the blest.

And the breezes, lightly blowing,
  Over deserts vast and drear,
Over rivers wilding flowing,
  Greetings out of Zion bear.
Balm the sweetest, too, they bring him,
  Balm from Zion's holy hill.
Melodies of home they sing him.
  Wakening every pulse's thrill.

———

Happy he, the world forgetting,
  Mid the tumult all around,
Who, his casement open setting,
  Looking Zionward is found ;
Who, beneath his burden bending,
  Lifts to heaven his bitter sigh.
Morn, and noon, and evening sending
  Messages of faith on high.

Though I had in fullest measure
  All that crowns the worldling's bliss,
Mines untold of richest treasure,
  Gardens of Semiramis ;
Still, with Babel's walls around me
  I should feel the tyrant's hand,
Long to break the chain that bound me,
  Hie me to the Fatherland.

Though in some deep dungeon pining
　I must dwell in darkest night,
Lo, a glory round me shining
　Fills the dungeon with its light,
As my heart its casement throwing
　Open towards the heavenly hills,
Somewhat of the light there glowing
　Falls, and all my being fills.

When 'mid cares which daily press me,
　Cares which none but I may wear ;
When the pains of life distress me,
　Pains so burdensome to bear,
Then my casement opening flinging
　Towards the lands by angels trod,
All my care and pain there bringing,
　Find I sweet relief in God.

When disease my frame is wasting,
　From Jerusalem the fair
Strength I draw, already tasting
　Daily of its blissful air.
Stars of hope, too, brightly burning
　O'er my pilgrim way appear ;
And the harpers, earthward turning,
　Waft a message to my ear.

Thus, where'er my home I make me,
　Here or far in distant lands,
Daily Zionward I take me,—
　Open wide my casement stands.
What though Babylon is ringing
　With the tumult of the street,
O'er it all my heart upspringing,
　Zion undisturbed I greet.

BE OF GOOD CHEER.

Be of good cheer, O soul !
   Angels are nigh :
Evil can harm thee not,
   God hears thy cry.

Into no void shalt thou
   Spring from this clay ;
His everlasting arm
   Shall be thy stay.

Day hides the stars from thee,
   Sense hides the heaven
Waiting the contrite soul
   That here has striven.

Soo n shall the glorydawn,
   Making earth dim ;
Be not disquieted,
   Trust thou in Him.

OUR THOUGHTS IN HEAVEN.

BY S. A. J.

We may soar above earth on the angelic wings
   Of fervent devotion and prayer,
And catch some faint glimpses of heavenly things,
   But what will our thoughts be when there ?

We will wish we had rolled every burden away
   On a faithful, omnipotent arm,
When we see that the Lord of the night and the
     day
   Himself was our shield from all harm.

We will never regret that we here loved His Word
　　And drank of the life-giving fount ;
When vista on vista of knowledge shall ope,
　　As we walk with our Lord on the mount.

We will wish that on earth, with a bountiful hand,
　　We had scattered the truth's holy seed,
When its fruit we behold in Immanuel's land,
　　As the labourer's glorious meed.

With joy had we borne every trial and loss,
　　And the fear of the world trampled down,
Had we seen that the darkest and heaviest cross
　　Would change to a star and a crown.

With what fervour had called in this valley of tears,
　　On our Lord, had we felt He would own
Our prayers as sweet incense from censer of gold,
　　Rising up as a cloud to His throne.

When we mourned for friends that were lost to our sight
　　With a bitter and heart-broken cry,
Our wail had been changed to an anthem of praise,
　　Had we seen but their glory on high.

Let us bring every thought of that light-beaming world
　　To bear as a lever on this,
And raise up the beings that sin has enthralled
　　To the height of that infinite bliss,

When we meet the freed spirits of saints that on earth,
　　With " affliction and iron " were bound

We shall wish we had loved, when of love they
· had need,
Whom Christ with His glory hath crown'd.

Their faces were marred, and their frail forms
were bowed,
And too often our hearts turned away ;
How we'll wish we had been as a light to their
eyes,
When no longer they sigh for the day !

We will wish we had meekly and patiently borne
With the frailties we saw in a friend,
Whom Christ in His tender compassion hath
kept,
And watched o'er and loved to the end ;

Had followed the Shepherd in seeking the sheep
Astray in the darkness and cold,
And when it was found, had rejoiced in His joy,
And gathered it safe in the fold.

Oh, how we shall wish when enraptured we stand
With our feet on the glorified shore,
And follow our Lord in the beautiful land,
That on earth we had loved Him far more.

Let us cling to these words as a silvery cord
To guide through the darkness of even,
We will do unto those whom Christ gives us to
aid,
As we'll wish when we meet them in heaven.

And oh, with what gladness of soul shall we serve
  The humblest whom Christ hath made free,
When we feel that the King at the judgment will
      say,
  " Fear not ; ye have done it to me." ·

———

OVER AND OVER AGAIN.

Over and over again,
  No matter which way I turn,
I always find in the Book of Life
  Some lessons I have to learn.
I must take my turn at the mill,
  I must grind out the golden grain,
I must work at my task with a resolute will
  Over and over again.

We cannot measure the need
  Of even the tiniest flower,
Nor check the flow of the golden sands
  That run through a single hour.
But the morning dew must fall,
  And the sun and the summer rain
Must do their part, and perform it all
  Over and over again.

Over and over again
  The brook through the meadow flows,
And over and over again
  The pond'rous mill-wheel goes.
Once doing will not suffice,
  Though doing be not in vain ;
And a blessing failing us once or twice,
  May come if we try again.

The path that has once been trod,
　　Is never so rough to feet ;
And the lesson we once have learned
　　Is never so hard to repeat.
Though sorrowful tears may fall,
　　And the heart to its depth be driven
With storm and tempest, we need them all
　　To render us meet for heaven.

INTO THE LIGHT.

BY M. C.

THE day was dark and cold and drear ;
　　Without, the raindrops falling
Kept time to sadder thoughts within,
　　My grief and pain recalling.

My eyes were wet with falling tears—
　　My lack of faith brought blindness,
God's way's seemed hard ; I could not see
　　He meant me only kindness.

And so I murmured more and more
　　And yielded to my sorrow ;
I longed to see each day depart,
　　And dreaded each to-morrow.

But God was watching o'er me still,
　　Through all my bitter railing ;
I turned to Him, and found again
　　His strength and grace unfailing.

" Thy will be done, O Lord ! " I cried,
　　" Forgive my long repining—
Thy will be done ! "　Lo ! all the world
　　Was like the noon-day shining.

THE GOSPEL OF MYSTERY.

BY SAXE HOLM.

GOOD tidings every day :
God's messengers ride fast.
    We do not hear one-half they say,
    There is such noise on the highway,
Where we must wait while they ride past.

    Their banners blaze and shine
With Jesus Christ's dear name,
    And story how by God's design,
    He saves us, in His love divine,
And lifts us from our sin and shame.

    Their music fills the air,
Their songs sing all of heaven ;
    Their ringing trumpet-peals declare
    What crowns to souls who fight and dare
And win, shall presently be given.

    Their hands throw treasures round
Among the multitude.
    No pause, no choice, no count, no bound,
    No questioning how men are found,
If they be evil or be good.

    But all the banners bear
Some words we cannot read ;
    And mystic echoes in the air,
    Which borrow from the songs no share,
In sweetness all the songs exceed.

And of the multitude,
No man but in his hand
    Holds some great gift misunderstood,
    Some treasure, for whose use or good
His ignorance sees no demand.

    These are the tokens lent,
By Immortality ;
    Birth-marks of our Divine descent :
    Sureties of ultimate intent,
God's Gospel of Eternity.

    Good tidings every day :
The messengers ride fast.
    Thanks be to God for all they say :
    There is such noise on the highway,
Let us keep still while they ride past.

THE HAVEN GAINED.

BY JANE M. READ.

BILLOWS in tumult, near the haven dashing,
    Toss, in their wrath, a vessel bound for home ;
Over its sides the rolling waves are plashing,
    Breaking and falling into spray and foam ;
Meeting near shore are tides of wondrous power,
    Each, in its pride, would rule the restless sea ;
Seamen are toiling through the midnight hour ;
    Danger is there, and awful majesty.
But, over all, that One His watch is keeping,
    Who, by His word, on storm-tossed Galilee,
Calmed all the tumult, waking from His sleeping,
    Chiding alike the tempest and the sea.

Reaching at length the welcome port, and gazing
    Fondly on happy homes along the shore,
God and His love the seaman's heart is praising,
    For at God's word the billows roll no more.
Fair was the landscape to the sailor, weary
    After his labour through the gloomy night;
After the danger, 'mid those shadows dreary,
    Glorious appeared that haven, bathed in light.

Fair is the harbour where the spirit, resting,
    Sings in its joy; the toil-worn Christian's home!
Meeting this side, two tides in strength contesting,
    Crown their vast billows white with seething
        foam;
Yet, though the billows o'er the soul are sweeping,
    Tempests shall rise no greater than our strength.
God at a word can change to joyous weeping—
    We shall behold our heavenly home at length.
And when the Christian sees the radiant morning
    Break on his sight, the haven gained at last,
Charmed with the glory, will he hail the dawning
    Brighter because of dangers bravely passed.

TRUST.

I CANNOT see, with my small human sight,
Why God should lead this way or that for me;
I only know He saith "Child, follow Me;"
    But I can trust.

I know not why my path should be at times
So straitly hedged, so strangely barred before;
I only know God could keep wide the door;
    But I can trust.

I find no answer, often, when beset
With questions fierce and subtle on my way,
And often have but strength to faintly pray;
   But I can trust.

I often wonder, as with trembling hand
I cast the seed along the furrowed ground,
If ripened fruit for God will there be found;
   But I can trust.

I cannot know why suddenly the storm
Should rage so fiercely round me in its wrath;
But this I know, God watches all my path
   And I can trust.

I may not draw aside the mystic veil
That hides the unknown future from my sight;
Nor know if for me waits the dark or light;
   But I can trust.

I have no power to look across the tide,
To know, while here, the land beyond the river;
But this I know, I shall be God's for ever;
   So I can trust.

VIA CRUCIS, VIA LUCIS.

BY MRS. C. A. MEANS.

THREE little graves beneath the sod,
Three sinless spirits safe with God;
A lonely pathway must be trod;
   She murmured not.

" God knows how heavy is the cross,
What anguish keen, what bitter loss,
How earthly treasures seem but dross ;
     He sees, *He* cares.

" No love my widowed heart can fill,
No joy the life-long craving still,
He knoweth best— it is His will,"
     She meekly said.

God's strength is given her cross to bear ;
She seeks another's grief to share,
And strives to lighten pain and care,
     Where'er she treads.

Is *thy* heart pierced with keenest woe ?
Then seek around thy path to throw
A heavenly light, which all may know,
     And own Divine.

ONLY.

BY JAMES F. STEARNS.

ONLY a poisonous drop from a cup,
  But it gave a thirst for more,
And awoke a craving that wrecked a life,
  On a barren, desert shore.

'Twas only a glance, but a scornful glance,
  And it fanned a dreaded flame.
It was only a kind, beseeching look,
  But it won a heart from shame.

It was only a dying mother's kiss
  On a fair, pale girlish face,
But always the thought of that sacred touch
  Drew her from evil apace.

'Twas only a draught from the limpid stream,
  But it saved the hunter's life.
'Twas only the husband's familiar step,
  Yet it cheered the gloomy wife.

It was only a smile—a pleading smile—
  But it reached a hardened heart,
And roused a desire and an earnest will
  To perform a noble part.

It was only a tear—one pearly tear—
  That stood on the maiden's cheek,
Yet it spoke a sweeter good-bye than words
  Have ever essayed to speak.

It was only a word—one single word—
  But sweet as the summer's breath,
And it touched the spring of a thoughtless mind,
  And rescued a soul from death.

TENEO ET TENEOR.

BY T. L. ROGERS.

I HOLD Thy truth, O Lord, within my heart ;
    Thy law I love ;
I hold Thy cross and try to do my part
    Its power to prove ;
I hold Thy promise, Lord, and daily pray
    My faith increase,
That I may closer cling to Thee, the way;
    And save Thy peace.

Yet little joy my holding brings to me,
     Because I know
That though full well I love my soul and Thee,
     I may let go.

But *I am held.* O Lord, Thou hast my hand,
     And Thou hast strength,
And on my journey in this desert land,
     Throughout its length,
Thy promise is to lead. I shall not fall,
     Though foes assail
And press me hard ; over myself and all
     I shall prevail ;
And so great joy Thy hold on me affords,
     Because I know
That Thou wilt not, according to Thy words,
     Of me let go.

MERCIES.

My meditation of Him shall be sweet.—*Psalm* 104, 34.

SHALL I tell you of what I've been thinking,
     And thinking the livelong day,
From the earliest dawn of the morning
     Till the sunset faded away,—

And on through the sweet, still evening,
     And into the starry night,
Till my soul is filled with music,
     And the way is all flooded with light ?

It is of the Lord's rich blessings,
     And His tender mercies I sing,
Thick as the fragrant blossoms
     In the wonderful, beautiful spring.

All fraught with grace and helping,
   They come straight down from above,
From the hand of the Heavenly Father,
   Whose very name is love.

Sometimes I can hardly see them,
   When doubts and fears assail ;
But 'tis only my blinded vision,
   And not that His mercies fail.

And sometimes they seem like sorrows,
   All fierce, and dark, and chill ;
But when I turn to the other side,
   The mercies are shining still.

Then what can I do but trust Him,
   Since he sends me what is best ?
And I know He's leading me safely
   To his own eternal rest !

THE ANSWER

To a question as to his belief in the eternity of punishment.

BY J. G. WHITTIER.

THOUGH God be good and free be Heaven,
   No force divine can love compel ;
And though the song of sins forgiven
   May sound through lowest hell,

The sweet persuasion of His voice
   Respects thy sanctity of will,
He giveth day, thou hast thy choice
   To walk in darkness still.

No word of doom may shut thee out,
   No wind of wrath may downward whirl,
No swords of fire keep watch about
   The open gates of pearl ;

A tenderer light than moon or sun,
   Than sung of earth a sweeter hymn,
May shine and sound forever on,
   And thou be deaf and dim.

Forever round the mercy seat
   The guiding lights of love shall burn ;
But what if, habit-bound, thy feet
   Shall lack the will to turn ?

What if thine eyes refuse to see,
   Thine ear of Heaven's free welcomefail,
And thou a willing captive be,
   Thyself thy own dark jail?

ROME, ABOVE AND BELOW.

BY EMILY SEAVER.

Up above, the churches, in their jewelled
    splendour,
   And wavering censers, with their rich perfume;
Down below, the rudely hewn-out arches,
   The cave-like chapels, and the mouldering
    gloom.

Up above, the ever-burning candles,
   And costly altars by their light displayed ;
Down below, the glaring of the lurid torches
   Shows where the saints in endless twilight
    prayed.

Above, the gaudy shrines of the Madonna,;
  Pictures of saints by kneeling crowds adored ;
Below, the fish, the dove, and the Good Shepherd,
  And simple altars where they sought the Lord.

Above, the worshipped relics of the martyrs,
  A thousand-fold, O wonder, multiplied ;
Below, the tomb, a rudely sculptured palm-
      branch,
  And words of praise to Jesus crucified.

Above, the daily, oft-repeated masses,
  For souls in torment, that their pain may cease;
Below, the simple, hopeful, sweet inscription,
  " He suffered and he sleeps ;" "He rests in peace."

O, that the spirit of the brave old martyrs
  Might fill the churches, walk the streets of
      Rome,
And we no more, amid the dust of ages,
  Need seek the Faith down in the Catacomb !

A BIT OF COUNSEL.

BY L. L. PHELPS.

Our life is like the ocean,
  With ebb, and tide, and flow,
And gems of choicest beauty,
  Hidden in depths below.

The varying tints of ocean,
  Now green, now gray, now blue,
Are only the reflection
  Of heaven's changeful hue.

While far beneath the surface,
  The turmoil and the strife,
Are regions calm and peaceful,
  Teeming with wondrous life.

From this a bit of counsel
  Is offered thee in love :
In every onward step of life,
  Keep thine eyes fixed above ;

And catching the reflection
  Of thy Father's smiling face,
Lining each cloud with glory,—
  Possess thy soul in peace.

E'en when the storms are raging
  Most fiercely o'er thy path,
Keep thy heart calm and peaceful,
  Unmoved by all their wrath.

Beneath the billows' dashing,
  Beyond the surges' roar,
Abide thyself in quiet,
  Where storms disturb no more.

Thus walking thou shalt lighten
  This life of many cares ;
And other hearts shall bless thee,—
  An angel unawares.

CHRIST.

BY E. R. G.

He came in gentlest pity,
  It seemed that I could see
My Father, ah, my Father,
  Bend down and look at me !

O, human heart of God in Christ.
O, pitying, patient heart of Christ,
   He pointed unto thee!

Thou seest all, Thou knowest all,
   The doubting and the sin ;
But more tender than my mother's love,
   Thy love that shuts me in.
O, so full of mercy is Thy love,
   That through that love I win !

A LESSON.

BY A. J. R.

SILENTLY, softly, o'er city and town,
Beautiful snowflakes came falling down.
Tiny crystals, so feathery light,
Covering the earth with a globe of white.

When I arose in the early dawn,
Brown earth and bare trees all were gone ;
Beauty and purity met my sight,
Silently wrought in the hours of night.

Looking abroad on a world so fair,
Read I the lesson written there,—
The bare, brown land, the homely soil,
Is the heart so stained by sin and toil.

The beautiful snow, so soft and white,
Is the grace of God as a robe of light ;
Noiselessly ever, it falls on the heart,
Clothing anew its every part.
Silently, softly, o'er city and town,
God's gift to the people, His grace, comes down.

BEYOND THE SUNSET.

BY METTIE BELLE CRANE.

FAR beyond the purpling mountains
  Golden clouds hang in the West ;
Twilight draws her mystic curtains,
  And the sun sinks to his rest.
Shadows o'er the earth are falling ;
  A soft silence o'er it lies,
As if an angel breathed thereon
  The sweet quiet of the skies.

Thus my earthly life is closing ;
  Soon will come the day's decline ;
But beyond the glorious morning
  Through the golden portals shine.
Shadows o'er my path are falling ;
  Earthly visions fade away :
But beyond the beauteous sunset
  Rises an eternal day.

On the golden steps of Heaven
  Cometh One I've longed to see ;
Soft and sweet as summer breezes
  Is His bidding, " Come to me."
Heaven opens to my vision,
  And the angels come and go,
And I think I hear among them
  Voices that I used to know.

Friends, and home, and love await me,
  Joys that never know decay,
In the land beyond the sunset,
  In a bright, eternal day.

Softly now the day is closing ;
   Evening shades are drawing nigh ;
To my glorious home I'm hastening—
   Is this death ? 'Tis sweet to die.

" THERE REMAINETH THEREFORE A REST."

BY S. R. L.

YES, I shall rest. When ? He knows best.
   When care and I lie down together.
The future morrow shall bring no sorrow,
   Nor wintry winds and stormy weather.

Safe from all harm, with folded palm,
   They'll bear me through the busy street ;
Cloudy or fair, I will not care,
   When I am borne to my retreat.

Perhaps the foe, with one dread blow,
   Will silence me in dreamless sleep.
What matter ? 'twill be my last ill,
   There are not many left to weep.

But this I pray, be when it may,
   By Thy atoning sacrifice,
O Saviour mine, Thou'lt own me Thine.
   Thy righteousness for all suffice.

Yes, I shall rest among the blest.
   After that sweet, untroubled sleep,
With tearless eyes, I will arise,
   To meet with those who never weep.

My soul, be lowly!   O live thou holy!
  With patience all endure,
Until, all glorious, I rise victorious
  Where Christ has gone before.

HEAVEN.

How sweetly strange will be the day
When we shall no more kneel and pray
For daily bread ; but wondering say,
  "We hunger now no more!"

When we shall hear the cooling rill,
And feel the fountain's freshness fill
The vital balmy air, and still
  Thirst not for ever more!

When we shall fly on errands vast ;
And pore o'er secret wonders past,
While heaven's revolving ages last,
  Yet we no older grow!

When we shall plan for endless years ;
And joy in God ; and know our fears
Lie in the sole tomb that appears,
  The tomb of all our woe!

When service shall be wrought aright,
Love the only motive ; O Thou Light!
For ever banishing the night,
  Thou shalt make all things new!

There Love unfurls her starry wings,
And pours her soul forth as she sings,
Untired as living water springs
  To shower melodious dew.

There, beckoning to some shining throne,
Our suffering darlings crowned, our own,
Shall fold us in a bliss unknown ;
　　The patient, tried, and true !

And if, obeying Love's command,
Among those ransomed ones shall stand
Some soul uplifted by our hand,
　　What praises will be due !

And oh ! to see our Saviour smile !
We being certain all the while
The sin that did our souls defile
　　And made us cry " Unclean "

Is blotted out ; as from the sky
When the great sun goes shining by,
Are the dark clouds that threat'ning lie !
　　As if they had not been !

So that He whom our souls adore
Can look us through, and o'er and o'er,
Nor find one stain for evermore ;
　　And we can look on Him.

Nor shrink, nor strive to hide, nor sigh ;
But find it Heaven's joy to lie
Full in the light of His pure eye,
　　Made pure like Him, by Him !

And now, though words must fail to tell
The whole of Heaven ; yet is it well
That Hope within the veil should dwell
　　And sing of the unseen.

GOOD THOUGHTS.

No man can safely go abroad that does not love to stay at home; no man can safely speak that does not willingly hold his tongue; no man can safely govern that would not cheerfully become subject; no man can safely command that has not truly learned to obey; and no man can safely rejoice but he that has the testimony of a good conscience.

WHEN I was a young man, there lived in our neighbourhood a farmer who was usually reported to be a very liberal man, and uncommonly upright in his dealings. When he had any of the produce of his farm to dispose of, he made it an invariable rule to give good measure—rather more than would be required of him. One of his friends, observing him frequently doing so, questioned him as to why he did it; he told him he gave too much, and said it would be to his disadvantage. Now, mark the answer of this excellent man :—

"God has permitted me but one journey through the world, and when I am gone I cannot return to rectify mistakes."

DID men govern themselves as they ought, instead of trying to govern each other, the world would be well disciplined.

The cradle of civilisation is rocked by a mother's hand.

———

Religion is not a mere debt we owe to God; it is a spirit of fellowship and sympathy with Him; it is the highest proof that God has made us for Himself, and redeemed us to Himself, and called us to be renewed in His image once more, and to be perfect as our Father in Heaven is perfect.

———

Christian faith is a grand cathedral, with divinely pictured windows. Standing without, you see no glory nor can possibly imagine any; standing within, every ray of light reveals a harmony of unspeakable splendours. — *Hawthorne.*

———

Neighbourly Love.—Genuine neighbourly love knows no distinction of persons. It is like the sun, which does not ask on what it shall shine, or what it shall warm; but shines and warms by the very laws of its own being. So there is nothing hidden from light and heat.

———

If in a dish of sand I should look with my eyes for the particles of iron, or feel for them with my fingers, I might be unable to detect them. But let me take a magnet and sweep through it, and how would it draw to itself the most invisible particles by the mere power of attraction! The unthankful heart, like the

fingers in the sand, discovers no mercies; but
let the thankful heart sweep through the day,
and as the magnet finds the iron, so it will find,
in every hour, some heavenly blessings; only the
iron in God's sand is gold.—*O. W. Holmes.*

IT is a very solemn thing to live, unless a man
is living right; and then it is a very joyful thing
to live.　It is a very solemn thing for a man to
die if he does not know where he is to go at
death; but it is a final triumph, and it may well
be an ecstacy, to the man whose conscience
bears him witness that all his purposes have been
just, and pure, and loving, and true.　Death to
him is only coronation and glory.—*Beecher.*

TEMPEST-TOSSED.

BY EGBERT L. BANGS.

MY soul this day is tempest-tossed,
　The winds around me madly blow,
And conscience thunders, " Thou art lost,
　Unless thy Saviour mercy show."
With terror wild my heart doth quake;
O sleeping Christ, within me wake!

My passions burn with furious heat,
　They drive me where I would not go;
Unholy pleasures lure my feet
　Where I sweet peace can never know.
Show me the path that I should take;
O sleeping Christ, within me wake!

As lightnings flash along the sky,
   And then the midnight darkness leave,
So anger lights my spirit high;
   In deepest penitence I grieve.
Let not my heart with anguish break;
O sleeping Christ, within me wake!

Thick clouds of doubt around me rise,
   No light comes to me from above;
They hide my Father from my eyes,
   And make me question His dear love.
I call to thee; for thy love's sake,
O sleeping Christ, within me wake!

Now hear me when I cry to thee,
   Bid passions' winds and waves be still;
Let light and peace come back to me,
   For they obey Thy holy will.
With terror wild my heart doth quake;
O sleeping Christ, within me wake!

THANKSGIVING.

BY C. B. L.

THE year began with gladness and a song—
Shall we rejoice because the tune went wrong?
      How can we give Thee thanks?

We reaped rich harvests but a year ago,
Now brown and barren all our fields lie low;
      Must we for this give thanks?

Our eyes are blinded by the tears we shed;
Beside a grave we sit discomforted;
    We see no place for thanks.

Our hearts are heavy while we stand and wait,
And we are hungry, poor, and desolate;
    Can this be time for thanks?

Because the discord only helped the strain,
As hearts grow tender through exceeding pain;
    For this we will give thanks.

Our fields lie fallow under rain and snow
Because the Husbandman works wisest so;
    And we will give Him thanks.

The heavy tears make lighter the heart's pain,
The bow of promise shines through falling rain;
    For that we give Thee thanks.

The heart whose food has longest been denied
Will be most grateful for their need supplied;
    For all we render thanks.

DO THY LITTLE.

Do thy little, do it well;
Do what right and reason tell;
Do what wrong and sorrow claim,
Conquer sin and cover shame.

Do thy little, though it be
Dreariness and drudgery;
They whom Christ apostles made
"Gathered fragments" when He bade.

Do thy little; never mind
Though thy brethren be unkind;
Though the men who ought to smile
Mock and taunt thee for a while.

Do thy little; never fear
While thy Saviour standeth near;
Let the world its javelins throw;
On thy way undaunted go.

Do thy little; God has made
Million leaves for forest shade;
Smallest stars their glory bring;
God employeth every thing.

AT THE GATE OF HEAVEN.

I'm kneeling at the threshold, weary, faint and
sore;
Waiting for the dawning, for the opening of the
door,
Waiting till the Master shall bid me rise and
come
To the glory of His presence, to the gladness of
His home.

A weary path I've travelled, 'mid darkness,
storm, and strife,
Bearing many a burden, struggling for my life;
But now the morn is breaking, my toil will soon
be o'er,
I'm kneeling at the threshold, my hand is on the
door.

Methinks I hear the voices of the blessed as
    they stand,
Singing in the sunshine of the sinless land ;
O, would that I were with them, amid their
    shining throng,
Mingling in their worship, joining in their song!

The friends that started with me have entered
    long ago ;
One by one they left me struggling with the foe.
Their pilgrimage was shorter, their triumph
    sooner won,
How lovingly they'll hail me when my toil is
    done.

With them, the blessed angels, that know not
    grief nor sin,
I see them by the portals, prepared to let me in.
O Lord, I wait Thy pleasure—Thy time and
    way are best ;
But I'm wasted, worn, and weary—O Father,
    bid me rest !

GOD'S QUIET.

There's silence in the holy place
    Where sits the Holiest on the throne,
And silence in the unmeasured space,
    Where silver stars go pacing on
Eternally, eternally.
    Around him moves the universe ;
Earth only breaks the harmony
    With her discordant curse.

Sad earth! whose music breaks in moans
  Against the crystal of the sky—
Poor earth; to have but bitter groans
  Wherewith to make reply.
All silently, all silently,
  Upon thee fall the light and dew!
God sends His blessings unto thee—
  Alas! His judgments, too.

Now, wherefore is the constant strife?
  And wherefore is the ceaseless moan?
Why does the dust of our low life
  Rise up in clouds before the throne?
Unceasingly, unceasingly,
  We vex His patience with our prayers;
For Him to rise and work, we cry;
  Impatient that He spares.

For Him to work; His chariot wheels
  Pause never in their onward way;
Even now before Him error reels;
  And yet we charge Him with delay!
All silently, all silently,
  He breaks the yoke, He gives the meed—
Calm, for His own eternity
  Hath time for any deed.

I think it is that we are weak—
  Our life so short, so faint our breath;
We find the feeble words we speak
  Strike blankly on the shore of death.
And yet they live eternally!
  They echo on a far off shore;
O mortals, know your destiny!
  Speak hopeless words no more.

God's great hereafter lieth bright
  Beyond life's valley, death's abyss;
A triumph crowns the perfect right
  Wherewith that world doth compass this.
In silence His eternity
  Flows round our little isle of life;
There's room for calm in that great sea—
  With us, for only strife.

ONLY A LITTLE CHILD.

BY MISS E. MARIA UPHAM.

Close by Thy side will I walk all day,
  Thou Holy One, meek and mild,
Lest from the narrow and blessed way,
Out in the cold and dark, I stray;
  For I'm only a little child.

Into Thy hand will I place my hand,
  Thy love hath my heart beguiled;
And I will believe Thou hast wisely planned
Things that I cannot now understand;
  For I'm only a little child.

Over the moorland cold and drear,
  Over the mountains wild,
I will never falter, or doubt, or fear,
With Thee and Thy tender love so near;
  Though I'm only a little child.

And when I am tired and long for rest,
  Thou Holy One meek and mild,
O, lift me up to Thy loving breast,
And tenderly whisper of home and rest;
  For I'm only a little child.

SHALL WE KNOW EACH OTHER THERE?

WHEN we hear the music ringing
　　Through the bright celestial dome,
When sweet angel voices singing
　　Gladly bid us welcome home
To the land of ancient story,
　　Where the spirit knows no care,
In the land of light and glory,
　　Shall we know each other there?

When the holy angels meet us,
　　As we go to join their band,
Shall we know the friends who greet us
　　In that glorious spirit land?
Shall we see the dark eyes shining
　　On us as in days of yore?
Shall we feel their dear arms twining
　　Fondly round us as before?

Yes, my earthworn soul rejoices
　　And my weary heart grows light,
For the thrilling angel voices
　　And the angel faces bright,
That shall welcome us in heaven,
　　Are the loved of long ago,
And to them is kindly given
　　Thus their mortal friends to know.

O, ye weary ones and lost ones,
　　Droop not, faint not, by the way!
Ye shall join the loved and lost ones
　　In the land of perfect day;

Harp-strings, touched by angel fingers,
　Murmur in my raptured ear ;
Evermore their sweet tone lingers,—
　We shall know each other there.

THE CHURCH AND THE WORLD.

BY MRS. M. C. EDWARDS.

THE Church and the World walked far apart,
　On the changing shore of time ;
The World was singing a giddy song,
　And the Church a hymn sublime.
"Come, give me your hand," cried the merry
　　World,
　"And walk with me this way."
But the good Church hid her snowy hand,
　And solemnly answered, "Nay,
I will not give you my hand at all,
　And I will not walk with you ;
Your way is the way to endless death ;
　Your words are all untrue."

"Nay, walk with me but a little space,"
　Said the World, with a kindly air.
"The road I walk is a pleasant road.
　The sun shines always there.
My path, you see, is a broad, fair one,
　And my gate is high and wide ;
There is room enough for you and for me
　To travel side by side."

Half shyly the Church approached the World
　And gave him her hand of snow,

The old World grasped it, and walked along,
    Saying in accents low :
" Your dress is too simple to please my taste :
    I'll give you pearls to wear,
Rich velvets and silks for your graceful form,
    And diamonds to deck your hair."
The Church looked down at her plain white robe,
    And then at the dazzling World,
And she blushed as she saw his handsome lip,
    With a smile contemptuous curled.

" I will change my dress for a costlier one,"
    Said the Church with a smile of grace.
Then her pure white garments drifted away,
    And the world gave in their place
Beautiful satin and shining silks,
    And roses and gems and pearls ;
And over her forehead her bright hair fell
    Crisped in a thousand curls.

" Your house is too plain," said the proud old
      World,
    " I'll build you one like mine—
Carpets of Brussels, and curtains of lace,
    And furniture ever so fine."
So he built her a costly and beautiful house,
    Splendid it was to behold ;
Her sons and her beautiful daughters dwelt there,
    Gleaming in purple and gold.
The Angel of Mercy flew over the Church,
    To gather the children in ;
But some were off at the midnight ball,
    And some were off at the play,
And some were drinking in gay saloons,
    So she quietly went her way.

Then the sly World gallantly said to her,
  "Your children mean no harm,
Merely indulging in innocent sports ; "
  So she leaned on his proffered arm,
And smiled and chatted, and gathered flowers,
  As she walked along with the World,
While millions and millions of deathless souls
  To the horrible gulf were hurled.

"You give too much to the poor," said the
    World ;
  " Far more than you ought to do.
If the poor need shelter, and food, and clothes,
  Why need it trouble you ?
Go, take your money and buy rich robes,
  And horses and carriages fine,
And pearls and jewels and dainty food,
  And the rarest and costliest wine.
My children they dote on all such things ;
  And if you their love would win,
You must do as they do, and walk in the ways
  That they are walking in."
Then the Church held tightly the strings of her
    purse,
  And gracefully lowered her head
And simpered, " I've given too much away :
  I'll do, sir, as you have said."

So the poor were turned from her door in scorn ;
  And she heard not the orphan's cry ;
And she drew her beautiful robes aside
  As the widows went weeping by.
And the sons of the World and the sons of the
    Church
  Walked closely hand and heart,

And only the Master, Who knoweth all,
  Could tell the two apart.

Then the Church sat down at her ease, and said,
  " I am rich and in goods increased
I have need of nothing, and naught to do
  But to laugh and dance and feast."
And the sly World heard her and laughed in his
      sleeve,
  And mockingly said aside :
The Church is fallen, the beautiful Church,
  And her shame is her boast and pride."

The Angel drew near to the mercy-seat,
  And whispered in sighs her name ;
And the saints their anthems of rapture hushed
  And covered their heads with shame.
And a voice came down through the hush of
      Heaven,
  From Him who sat on the throne,
" I know thy works, and how thou hast said
  I am rich ; and hast not known
That thou art naked, poor, and blind,
  And wretched before My face ;
Therefore, from My presence I cast thee out,
  And blot thy name from its place."

THE INWARD CHRIST.

BY T. C. UPHAM.

THE outward word is good and true,
But inward power alone makes new ;
Not even Christ can cleanse from sin,
Until He comes and works within.

I

It was for this He could not stay,
But hastened up the starry way ;
And keeps from outward sight apart,
That men may seek Him in the heart.

Christ in the heart ! if absent there
Thou canst not find Him anywhere ;
Christ in the heart ! O friends ! begin
And build the throne of Christ within,

And know from this that He is thine,
And that thy life is made Divine,
When holy love shall have control,
And rule supremely in the soul.

"MADE IN HIS IMAGE."

BY ANNIE E. JOHNSON.

MADE in His image.   Like a child
　That seeks its father's face,
But wanders, weary, through the earth
　Finding no resting-place,
Watching with eyes through sorrow dim,
　Pining to catch one smile from Him.

So pine our souls for Thee, our God !
　So thirst our spirits for Thy rest !
With faltering steps our feet have trod
　This lonely earth of Thee in quest ;
Give us Thy rest—give us Thy peace,
　So shall our weary longings cease !

"Made in His image."   Can it be
　That we have fallen so far !

How could we turn our gaze from Thee,
  Our bright and morning star !
O, be Thine own to Thee restored,
  And keep them in Thine image, Lord !

THE ANGEL WITH THE UPWARD LOOK.

BY L. I. PHELPS.

An angel with an upward look
  Walks ever at my side,
  With face that changes never,
  With footsteps turning ever
  To that glad, bright Forever,
Where breaks full memory's tide
    Upon the Past.

The angel with the upward look
  Oft leads my soul away ;
  From the past she turneth
  While my spirit yearneth
  For the things she spurneth,
Whispering of a brighter day
    Than the Past.

That angel with the upward look
  More radiant grows each day ;
  More of heaven in her face,
  More of wonder-working grace,
  And with her I calmly trace
Every sorrow-laden way
    Of the Past.

O angel of the upward look,
  I thank my God for thee.
Though my idols oft be crushed,
Though they crumble into dust,
Teach me still thy holy trust,
Evermore abide with me,
      Till all's past.

WAIT AND SEE.

WHEN my boy, with eager questions,
  Asking how, and where, and when,
Taxing all my store of wisdom,
  Asking o'er and o'er again
Questions oft to which the answers
  Give to others still the key,
I said, to teach him patience,
  "Wait, my little boy, and see."
And the words I taught my darling
  Taught to me a lesson sweet ;
Once, when all the world seemed darkened
  And the storm about me beat,
In the "children's room" I heard him,
  With a child's sweet mimicry,
To a baby brother's questions
  Saying wisely, "Wait and see."
Like an angel's tender chiding
  Came the darling's words to me,
Though my Father's ways were hidden,
  Bidding me still wait and see.
What are we but restless children,
  Ever asking what shall be ?
And the Father, in His wisdom,
  Gently bids us "wait and see."

THE CHRISTIAN CLOCK.

BY C. A. C.

" Alackaday !
The clock is a-ticking life's minutes away."

CHRISTAIN, hast thou ticked the hours,
  Moments, seconds, as they flew ?
Has thy soul with all its powers
  Kept thy faith and duty true ?

Dost thou keep good time for others
  Ever in thy lot and place ?
Do thine hands uphold thy brothers,
  Running fair the Christian race ?

Art thou working for the Master,
  Whose dear love thy soul possessed
With the joy of full salvation
  When the faith His name confessed ?

Are thy tones of love heard ever,
  Striking clear a silver chime,
As the hours, like watching angels,
  Mark the " dial-plate of time " ?

Is their record pure and glowing
  Of thy Christian life away ?
Art thou reaping, art thou sowing,
  Ticking true from day to day ?

" Have not ticked for months," you answer,
  Works run down, with rust strewn o'er,
Rusted wheels and long inaction,
  Past and present, you deplore.

Rise then ; wake to life and motion ;
  Use the golden key of prayer ;
Wind the soul to true devotion ;
  Keep thy deeds and records fair.

Then will faith and love in union
  Help thee to " redeem the time,"
And with Christ in true communion,
  Make thy earthy life sublime

THE BEAUTIFUL.

BY CLARA B. HEATH.

THERE'S something beautiful in every flower !
  Perhaps a crimson glow or pearly leaf ;
  Or, may it be a tint of Heaven's own blue,
  Or burnished shade like sunbeams shining
      thro'—
Something that whispers of a higher Power,
  And checks our unbelief.

There's something beautiful in every clime !
  A tropic growth to fascinate and charm ;
  A wild luxuriance, a wealth of vines,
  Curtained recesses where the sun ne'er shines,
Ripe, luscious berries,—a long summer's time
  Of summer rest and calm.

There's something beautiful in frost that bars
  The lakes and pools in caverns dark and still ;
  In the light clouds of fleecy falling snow,
  In the white fields whose wealth is hid below,
In the bright glitter of the pale, cold stars,
  Beyond our reach or will.

And is there not within the human heart—
  Deep down, perhaps within its lowest deep—
Some holy thought born great and beautiful?
Some worthy purpose, which, considered well,
And brought to its maturity, would start
  The soul from guilty sleep?

Why do we cover up these precious things,
  And crowd them down and smother them
      with sighs?
Why do we let the work-day world control,
Till all the life grows formal, dead and dull?
Why do we clip our own God-given wings,
  Till they no more can rise?

GIFTS.

BY C. M. WEDGWOOD.

If you'd bring me the treasures, New Year,
  That the Old Year has taken away,
You would make me happy and proud
  With your gifts each wonderful day.
I am looking for something now;
  A gift that will always be new.
Is there such a thing for me, New Year?
  O answer me, answer me true!

Not a book—I am weary of books;
  Not a ring—it will only be lost.
A flower? 'tis a beautiul thing,
  But will die in the pitiless frost.
It is hard to please me, I know,
  And yet I want only just this—
That it cannot be lost or grow old;
  It is sad if my gift I must miss.

And to think of the gifts I have lost,
  Sweet friends—true as steel—gone away.
Not one such is left to me now!
  Dark hairs—shining eyes—you are gray,!
I am tired to death.   What's the use
  Of expecting a present at all ?
This year will be just like the rest—
  Ice now, rain and wind in the fall.

A knock!   Who is there at the door ?
  I cannot see anyone now.
Must He come?   O who is He, and what
  Are the scars on His fair, kingly brow?
Come in, peace to Thee, Blessed One,
  My Lord, now I know Who Thou art
By the splendour that shines in my room,
  By the calm, loving trust in my heart !

No friend that is true, did I say ?
  My Saviour ! I thought not of Thee !
Lost Youth ?   Why the ages to come
  Have no moan for the days behind me !
Happy Year !   If He keep me in peace
  For the trust I have put in His name—
And He will—He hath promised, this year
  And the others will not be the same.

PRAYERS I DON'T LIKE.

I DO not like to hear him pray,
  Who loans at twenty-five per cent. ;
For then I think the borrower may
  Be pressed to pay for food and rent ;

And in the Book we all should heed,
  Which says the lender shall be blest,
As sure as I have eyes to read
  It does not say " Take interest."

I do not like to hear him pray
  On bended knees, about an hour,
For grace to spend aright the day,
  Who knows his neighbour has no flour.
I'd rather see him go to mill,
  And buy the luckless brother bread,
And see his children eat their fill,
  And laugh beneath their humble shed.

I do not like to hear him pray,
  " Let blessings on the widow be,"
Who never seeks her home to say,
  " If want o'ertakes you, come to me."
I hate the prayer, so loud and long,
  That's offered for the orphan's weal,
By him who sees him crushed by wrong,
  And only with the lips doth feel.

I do not like to hear her pray,
  With jewelled ear and silken dress,
Whose washerwoman toils all day,
  And then is asked to " work for less."
Such pious shavers I despise !
  With folded hands and face demure,
They lift to heaven their " angel eyes,"
  Then steal the earning of the poor.

I do not like such soulless prayers ;
  If wrong, I hope to be forgiven ;
No angel's wing them upward bears—
  They're lost a million miles from heaven.

A PRAYER FOR PURITY.

BY A. J. BATES.

WE would be loving and true, Father,
　We fain would live nearer to thee ;
But something stands in our way, Father,
　O help us, whatever it be !

Whatever that suffering may be, Father,
　Be it hatred, or passion, or pride,
From our hearts help us drive it, O Father,
　And let Jesus and love there abide.

In the darkness be with us, O Father !
　We cannot walk safely alone,
But if Thou wilt walk with us, Father,
　While for every sin we atone,—

We shall grow to be better and stronger ;
　Shall not be afraid by the way ;
We shall walk in the darkness no longer,
　For Thou leadest from night unto day.

Wherever we wander, dear Father,
　By mountain, or woodland, or stream,
The lesson is always the same, Father,
　We read it as one in a dream.

We read of Thine infinite love, Father,
　We see it displayed everywhere,
From the flowers that grow in the field, Father,
　From the birds that fly in the air,—

From the snow that rests on the mountains,
  From the rain that cools the fierce heat,
To the stream that flows from the Fountain
  Of Grace at Immanuel's feet !

May the Water of Life fill our hearts, Father,
  May it purge us from sin and from pride,
Till in heaven, our mission here over,
  We stand with the pure at Thy side.

LOVE AND LIFE.

BY MRS. ZADEL D. BUDDINGTON.

LIFE is like a stately temple
  That is founded in the sea,
Whose uprising fair proportions
  Penetrate immensity ;
Love the architect who builds it,
  Building it eternally.

To me, standing in the Present,
  As one waits beside a grave,
Up the aisles and to the altar
  Rolls the Past its solemn wave,
With a murmur as of mourning,
  Undulating in the nave.

Pallid phantoms glide around me
  In the wrecks of hope and home ;
Voices moan among the waters,
  Faces vanish in the foam ;
But a peace divine, unfailing,
  Writes its promise in the dome.

Cold the waters where my feet are,
  But my heart is strung anew,
Tuned to Hope's profound vibration,
  Pulsing all the ether through,
For the seeking souls that ripen
  In a patience strong and true.

Hark ! the all-inspiring Angel
  Of the future leads the choir ;
All the shadows of the temple
  Are illumed with living fire,
And the bells above are waking
  Chimes of infinite desire.

For the strongest or the weakest
  There is no eternal fall ;
Many graves and many mourners,
  But at last—the lifted pall !
For the highest and the lowest
  Blessed life containeth all.

O thou fair, unfinished temple !
  In unfathomed sea begun,
Love, thy builder, shapes and lifts thee
  In the glory of the sun ;
And the builder and the builded
  To the pure in heart—are one.

NATIONAL.

A STATEMENT, A PRAYER, AND A PROPHECY.

One-eighth of the whole population were coloured slaves, not distributed generally over the Union, but localised in the southern part of it. These slaves constituted a peculiar and powerful interest. All knew that this interest was, somehow, the cause of the war. To strengthen, perpetuate, and extend this interest was the object for which the insurgents would rend the Union, even by war; while the Government claimed no right to do more than to resist the territorial enlargement of it. Neither party expected for the war the magnitude or the duration which it has already attained. Neither anticipated that the *cause* of the conflict might cease with, or even before, the conflict itself should cease. Each looked for an easier triumph, and a result less fundamental and astounding. Both read the same Bible, and pray to the same God; and each invokes His aid against the other. It may seem strange that any men should dare to ask a just God's assistance in wringing their bread from the sweat of other men's faces ; but let us judge not, that we be not judged. The prayer of both could not be answered—that of neither has been answered fully. The Almighty has His own purposes. "Woe unto the world because of offences ; for it must needs be that offences come ; but woe to that man by whom the offence cometh." If we shall suppose that American slavery is one of those offences which, in the providence of God, must needs come, but which, having continued through His appointed time, He now wills to remove, and that He gives to both North and South this terrible war, as the woe due to those by whom the offence came, shall we discern therein any departure from those divine attributes which the believers in a living God always ascribe to Him ! Fondly do we hope—fervently do we pray —that this mighty scourge of war may speedily pass away. Yet, if God wills that it continue until all the wealth piled by the bondsman's two hundred and fifty years of unrequited toil shall be sunk, and until every drop of blood drawn with the lash shall be paid by another drawn with the sword, as was said three thousand years ago, so still it must be said, " The judgments of the Lord are true, and righteous altogether." With malice towards none, with charity for all, with firm ness in the right, as God gives us to see the right, let us strive on to finish the work we are in ; to bind up the nation's wounds ; to care for him who shall have borne the battle, and for his widow, and his orphan—to do all which may achieve and cherish a just and a lasting peace among our- selves and with all nations.—From *Abraham Lincoln's Last Inaugural Address.*

ABRAHAM LINCOLN.

BY R. H. STODDARD.

THIS man, whose homely face you look upon,
  Was one of Nature's masterful, great men ;
Born with strong arms, that unfought battles
    won :
  Direct of speech and cunning with the pen.

Chosen for large designs, he had the art
  Of winning with his humour, and he went
Straight to his mark, which was the human heart :
  Wise, too, for what he could not break, he bent.

Upon his back a more than Atlas-load,
  The burthen of the Commonwealth was laid ;
He stooped, and rose up to it, though the road
  Shot suddenly downwards, not a whit dismayed.

Hold, warriors, councillors, kings !—all now give
    place
To this dear benefactor of the Race !

JEFFERSON DAVIS.

[The following lines were written by a Northern " mudsill
  —a porter in the store of one of our friends —and we
  print them as evidence of the deep conviction of the
  great middling-class of our people.]

YOU rebelled, Mr. Davis, that you might prolong
To indefinite length the great national wrong ;
And, all red from the field with our countrymen
    strewn,
You so modestly asked us to let you alone !

And the friends of oppression all over the world,
Taking hope as they saw thy dark banner.
    unfurled,
Caught the pitiful din of that innocent tone,
And they all echoed back, "They must let you
    alone!"

Ay! so grandly that chorus swept over thy plains
That the Toms and Elizas forgot their rude
    chains;
And the wake with bright dreams of the future
    was strewn,
And the banjoes resounded, "They must let us
    alone!"

That response filled the air with its heart-stirring
    thrills,
And the glad breezes wafted them back to our
    hills,
To the men ever ready their brothers to own,
And the bugles and drums sounded, "Let them
    alone!"

So, although the foul tares you expected to reap
In the unwilling soil of good providence sleep,
Still the land is all golden with wheat you have
    sown,
And the heavens are ringing with, "Let them
    alone!"

You indeed raised the whirlwind in dreadfullest
    form,
But a stronger than you is directing the storm;
For, if laurels for Lincoln but slowly have blown,
The great God of the wronged hath not let thee
    alone!

All applause to the patient and spirited braves
That are pressing your place from the back of
 the slaves !
All applause to the widows and mothers that
 moan
While the cannons are thundering, "Let them
 alone !"

The dark night, Mr. Davis, will soon pass away,
And we trust there remains but a moment's
 delay ;
While Aurora embroiders her roseate zone
With the beautiful motto of, " Let me alone !"

And when comes that proud morn we are long-
 ing to see,
When this land shall indeed be the land of the
 free,
As the Queen of the Nations ascends to her
 throne,
She will move to the music of, " Let me alone !"

MAGNANIMITY LEE.

BY AN OLD FARMER.

HAVE ye heard of the mag-na-nim-i-tee
Of the great Suthern juntleman, Gineral Lee ?
I'm a plain old citizen, friends, I am,
And for words, as they go, I don't care a—clam ;
But none of your smoothed-up talk to me
Of Gineral Magnanimity Lee !

Wasn't he most mag-nan-i-*mouse*
When he tried to gnaw into our national house ;·

K

When he planted the shot of his murderus guns
Strait into the hearts of our brothers and sons ?
Has he follerd the bizness of throat-cutlery,
Sustained by his mag-na-nim-i·tee ?

If I had an ox that was goring his mate,
And rippin up things at a *re*bellious rate,
And ox number 2 got the better o' him—
Would I name the bad critter my old *Mag-na-
　　nim ?*
In the village I come from the thing we *don't* see
Is the *pre*cise mag-na-nim-i-tee !

We think it's a leetle too much out o' jint,
Arter schoolin young Lee up there at West Pint
Free gratis for nothin, with clothing and feed,
And teachin the lad how to sifer and reed,
To have him turn round with *jest* such a gee—
Or is it his mag-na-nim-i-tee ?

Wasn't it Christian for him to jine hans
With our Gineral Scott, and steal all his plans,
Then cut out and run to the foul rebel nest
With the whole Union program for stoppin the
　　pest !
My eyes have grown dim, for I really can't see
Robert's wonderful mag-na-nim-i-tee !

To tear down and keep down the old Union flag,
And hist up, instid of it, Slavery's rag,
To stamp on our freedom with red treason's noise,
And starve by the thousan our poor prisoner
　·　boys—

I'm a plain man, Captain, but it does seem to me
That this is *not* mag-na-nim-i-tee

And that other chap so pious and trew
That was squatting last Sunday so snug in his
    pew—
Where's Jeff. Davis hidin his brainy gray head
That planned all the mis'ry and piled up the
    dead
Betraying old Judas ! I wonder if he
Will set up *his* mag-na-nim-i-tee ?

Did it ever strike you how this sort o' cant
Would read in his tent to a fellow like Grant ?
How Butler would twist it to light his sheroot,
And Sheridan spurn it aside with his boot ?
Can't you hear the swift cuss of the brave-hearted
    three
As they take in the *mag-na-nim-i-tee !*

By thunder ! it makes us country folks swear
To hear people plarster the traitors down there ;
We've jest but one way ; it's to cave in the hive,
And pull out the sting from each rebel alive—
Or you may hear agin from more Robert Lees
With their usual mag-na-nim-i-tees !

Don't gloss over now that terrible night
When the traitors made havoc, and stabbed left
    and right !
Don't say that sech deeds as we shudder to tell
Belong to great heroes and not to deep hell !
They've killed Abram Lincoln ! just God ! can
    it be
That *treason* is mag-na-nim-i-tee ?

PSALM OF WAR.

BY HENRY PYMN.

"And Moses said 'Shall your brethren go to war, and
shall ye sit here?'"—NUMB. 32, 6.

I.

GIVE us War, O Lord !
Give us War !
Let its thunder and lightning break,
Forever and ever around us,
Till it cleanse and purify us,
Till its red, red rain of blood,
Of fire, of tears, and of blood,
Shall cleanse our land of sin—
Shall make us clean forever.
From a foul devouring ulcerous sore
Make us sweet and pure forever.
Our measure of guilt is full.
Give us War, O Lord !
Give us War !

II.

Give us wounds, O Lord,
Give us wounds !
Oh ! prisons and hunger and wounds !
Take our limbs, and enlarge our souls—
Give us freer, braver souls -
Till they burst the shell of a frivolous life,
A selfish, aimless, wasted life.
Take our limbs and make us larger men.
Give us wounds, O Lord,
Give us wounds !

III.

Give us Death, O God,.
Give us Death !
From our perishing lives uplift us !
From our shrivelling low self-seeking !
From our lying cowardly living !
Till for Land and Law and Liberty,
And the rights of the wronged who are weaker
than we,
Our lives shall be earnest pledges.
Give us Death, O God,
Give us Death !

IV.

What is Death, O Lord,
What is Death ?
Shame to the man who fears it,
Honour to him who scorns it,
A little bodily hurt,
For a space a little pain,
And then thy fresher kingdoms,
And all the loved departed,
Who watch and await us ever !
Our brothers have made it easy !
What is Death, O, Lord,
What is Death ?

V.

What is Life, O Lord,
What is Life ?
What is Life but noble action ;
Ho brothers ! hand in hand
Let us fly where danger is thickest,
Where the fight is closest and thickest

For there our country implores us
To come with our hearts and our bodies ;
The home ones urge us thither,
And there is the joy of the brave man.
Let us charge the mouths of cannon !
Let us sweep like a surge their bayonets!
What is life but noble action,
  What is Life, O Lord,
  What is Life?

VI.

  What is Love, O Lord,
  What is Love ?
What is Love but entire devotion ?
O maid ! stay not thy lover,
O friend ! stay not thy brother,
O wife ! give the heart newly wedded,
O mother ! the first of thy bosom.
Baptise them with tears, but take not away
From their lips the cup God presses to-day,
Of action and honour and glory.
What is love but entire devotion,—
  What is love, O Lord,
  What is Love?

VII.

  Give us Peace, O Lord,
  Give us Peace !
But ah ! peace that shall first be pure.
For the wicked no peace, O Lord.
Give us friends, ere we have won them,
Wife and child, ere worthy of them,
This bright star ere we become it,
Give us heaven ere we deserve it,

But never till we are pure—
From a public crime and shame all pure—
Give us Peace, O Lord,
Give us Peace.

WHAT THE BIRDS SAID.

BY JOHN G. WHITTIER.

THE birds, against the April wind,
Flew Northward, singing as they flew;
They sang, " The land we leave behind
Has swords for corn-blades, blood for dew."

" O wild birds, flying from the South,
What saw and heard ye, gazing down?"
" We saw the mortar's upturned mouth,
The sickened camp, the blazing town!

"Beneath the bivouacs starry lamps,
We saw your march-worn children die;
In shrouds of moss, in cypress swamps,
We saw your dead uncoffined lie.

"We heard the starving prisoner's sighs;
And saw, from line and trench, your sons
Follow our flight with home-sick eyes,
Beyond the battery's smoking guns."

" And heard and saw ye only wrong
And pain," I cried, " O wing-worn flocks?"
" We heard," they sang, " the Freedman's song,
The crash of Slavery's broken locks!

"We saw from new, uprising States
The Treason-nursing mischief spurned,

As, crowding freedom's ample gates,
  The long-estranged and lost returned.

"O'er dusky faces, seamed and old,
  And hands horn-hard with unpaid toil,
With hope in every rustling fold,
  We saw your star-dropt flag uncoil.

"And, struggling up through sounds accursed,
  A grateful murmur clomb the air,
A whisper scarcely heard at first,
  It filled the listening Heavens with prayer.

"And sweet and far, as from a star,
  Replied a voice which shall not cease,
Till, drowning all the noise of war,
  It sings the blessed songs of peace !"

So to me, in a doubtful day
  Of chill and slowly-greening Spring,
Low stooping from the cloudy grey,
  The wild birds sang or seemed to sing.

They vanished in the misty air,
  The song went with them in their flight ;
But lo ! they left the sunset fair,
  And in the evening there was light.

GOD NEVER MADE A SLAVE.

W. G. SNETHEN, A NEGRO.

COLUMBIA'S sons, though slaves ye be,
God your Creator made you free,
He life to all and being gave,
But never never, made a slave !

His works are wonderful to see,—
All, all proclaim the Deity ;
He made the earth, and formed the wave,
But never, never made a slave !

He made the skies with spangles bright,
The moon to shine by silent night,
The sun, and spread the vast concave,
But never, never made a slave !

The verdant earth on which we tread
Was by His hand all carpeted ;
Enough for all He freely gave,
But never, never made a slave !

All men are equal in his sight,
The bond, the free, the black, the white ;
He made them all, them freedom gave,
He made the man, man made the slave !

UNIVERSAL EMANCIPATION.

BY J. G. WHITTIER.

Thy hill-tops, New England, shall leap at the cry,
And the prairie and far-distant West shall reply
It shall roll o'er the land till the furtherest glen
Gives back the glad summons again and again.

Oppression shall hear in its temple of blood,
And read on its walls the handwriting of God ;
Niagara's torrents shall thunder it forth ;
It shall burn in the sentinel-star of the North.

It shall blaze in the lightning and speak in the
    thunder,
Till Slavery's fetters are riven asunder,
And Freedom her rights has triumphantly won,
And our country her garments of beauty put on.

The forests shall hear it, and lift up their voice,
And bid the green prairies and valleys rejoice ;
And the Father of Waters join Mexico's sea
In the anthem of Nature for millions set free !

GOD MARCHING ON.

BY JULIA WARD HOWE.

MINE eyes have seen the glory of the coming of
    the Lord ;
He is trampling out the vintage, where the grapes
    of wrath are stored ;
He has loosed the fateful lightning of his terrible
    swift sword ;
        His truth is marching on.

I have seen Him in the watch-fires of a hundred
    circling camps ;
They have builded Him an altar in the evening
    dews and damps ;
I can read His righteous sentence by the dim
    and flaring lamps,
        His day is marching on.

I have read a fiery gospel, writ in burnished rows
    of steel :
As ye deal with My contemners, so with you My
    grace shall deal ;

Let the Hero, born of woman, crush the serpent
    with his heel,
        Since God is marching on.

He has sounded forth the trumpet that shall
    never call retreat ;
He is sifting out the hearts of men before His
    judgment-seat ;
O ! be swift, my soul, to answer Him ! be jubi-
    lant, my feet !
        Our God is marching on.

In the beauty of the lilies Christ was borne across
    the sea,
With a glory in His bosom that transfigures you
    and me ;
As He died to make men holy, let us die to
    make men free,
        While God is marching on.

THE MOWER IN OHIO.

BY JOHN JAMES PIATT.

THE bees in the clover are making honey, and I
    am making my hay ;
The air is fresh, I seem to draw a young man's
    breath to-day.

The bees and I are alone in the grass, the air is
    so very still,
I hear the dam, so loud, that shines beyond the
    sullen mill.

Yes, the air is so still that I hear almost the
　　　sounds I cannot hear—
That, when no other sound is plain, ring in my
　　　empty ear.

The chime of striking scythes, the fall of the
　　　heavy swathes they sweep—
They ring about me, resting, when I waver half
　　　asleep ;

So still I am not sure if a cloud, low down, un-
　　　seen there be,
Or if something brings a rumour home of the
　　　cannon so far from me :

Far away in Virginia, where Joseph and Grant,
　　　I know,
Will tell them what I meant when first I bade
　　　my mowers go !

Joseph, he is my eldest one, the only boy of my
　　　three
Whose shadow can darken my door again, and
　　　lighten my heart for me.

Joseph, he is my eldest, how his scythe was strik-
　　　ing ahead !
William was better at short heats, but Jo in the
　　　long run led.

William, he was my youngest ; John, between
　　　them, I somehow see,
When my eyes are shut, with a little board at
　　　his head in Tennessee.

But William came home one morning early, from
    Gettysburg, last July
(The mowing was over already, although the only
    mower was I);

William, my captain, come home for good to his
    mother ; and I'll be bound
We were proud, and cried to see the flag that
    wrapt his coffin around ;

For a company from the town came up ten miles
    with music and gun ;
It seemed his country claimed him then—as well
    as his mother her son.

But Joseph is yonder with Grant to-day, a thou-
    sand miles or near,
And only the bees are abroad at work with me
    in the clover here.

Was it a murmur of thunder I heard that hummed
    again in the air?
Yet, may be, the cannon are sounding now their
    onward to Richmond there.

But under the beech by the orchard, at noon, I
    sat an hour it would seem—
It may be I slept a minute too, or wavered into
    a dream ;

For I saw my boys, across the field, by the flashes
    as they went,
Tramping a steady tramp as of old, with the
    strength in their arms unspent ;

Tramping a steady tramp, they moved like soldiers
    that marched to the beat
Of music that seems a part of themselves, to rise
    and fall with their feet ;

Tramping a steady tramp, they came with flashes
    of silver that shone,
Every step, from their scythes that rang as if they
    needed the stone—

(The field is wide and heavy with grass)—and
    coming toward me, they beamed
With a shine of light in their faces at once, and
    —surely I must have dream'd !

For I sat alone in the clover field, the bees were
    working ahead,
There were three in my vision—remember, old
    man ; and what if Joseph were dead !

But I hope that he and Grant (the flag above them,
    both, to boot)
Will go into Richmond together, no matter which
    is ahead or afoot !

Meantime alone at the mowing here—an old man
    somewhat gray—
I must stay at home as long as I can, making
    myself the hay.

And to another round—the quail in the orchard
    whistle blithe—
But first I'll drink at the spring below, and whet
    again my scythe.

LAUS DEO.

BY JOHN G. WHITTIER.

On hearing the bells ring for the Constitutional
Amendment abolishing Slavery in the
United States.

IT is done!
Clang of bell and roar of gun
Send the tidings up and down.
How the belfries rock and reel,
How the great guns, peal on peal,
Fling the joy from town to town!

Ring, O, bells!
Every stroke exulting tells
Of the burial-hour of crime.
Loud and long, that all may hear,
Ring for every listening ear
Of Eternity and Time!

Let us kneel:
God's own voice is in that peal,
And this spot is holy ground.
Lord forgive us! What are we,
That our eyes this glory see,
That our ears have heard the sound?

For the Lord
On the whirlwind is abroad;
In the earthquake He has spoken;
He has smitten with His thunder
The iron walls asunder,
And the gates of brass are broken!

Loud and long
Lift the old exulting song,
Sing with Miriam by the sea :
    He has cast the mighty down ;
    Horse and rider sink and drown ;
He has triumphed gloriously !

Did we dare,
In our agony of prayer,
Ask for more than He has done?
    When was ever His right hand
    Over any time or land
Stretched as now beneath the sun ?

How they pale,
Ancient myth, and song, and tale,
In this wonder of our days,
    When the cruel rod of war
    Blossoms white with righteous law,
And the wrath of man is praise !

Blotted out !
All within and all about
Shall a fresher life begin ;
    Freer breathe the universe,
    As it rolls its heavy curse
On the dead and buried sin !

It is done !
In the circuit of the sun
Shall the sound thereof go forth.
    It shall bid the sad rejoice,
    It shall give the dumb a voice,
It shall belt with joy the earth !

Ring and swing,
Bells of joy ! on morning's wing
Send the song of praise abroad ;
With a sound of broken chains
Tell the nation that He reigns
Who alone is Lord and God !

A SONG FOR THE TIMES.

BY W. H. FURNESS.

YOU all have heard of old John Brown,
A man he was right up and down,
Who, when he saw a thing was true,
Went straight to work to put it through,
    Put it through.

He took good care to count the cost,
How much there might be gained or lost,
And found, he said, that either way
The plan he had was sure to pay,
    Sure to pay.

The wise ones called John Brown a fool
Because he kept the Golden Rule :
What he wished you for him to do,
He was at hand to do for you,
    Do for you.

What bad men make to pass for Law
With old John Brown weighed not a straw,
And though enforced with all their might,
Shook not his faith that Right is right,
    Right is right.

L

It worked like madness in his brain
To see his brother drag a chain,
And, let him who would forbid or scoff,
Straight goes John Brown to strike it off,
           Strike it off.

The slaves were black, but none the less
His soul was moved by their distress ;
He never stopt to mind the skin,
But only saw the soul within,
           The soul within ;

Saw all their wrongs and all their shame,
Felt for the bound as bound with them,
Far better he were in his grave
Than live and never help the slave,
           Help the slave.

To stay his hand, to shut his mouth,
They seized and hung him in the South.
His mouth is hushed, his hand is still,
But old John Brown they could not kill,
           Could not kill.

For now the soul of old John Brown
From North and West comes marching down,
With wild hurrahs and roll of drums
And roar of cannon, lo, it comes !
           Lo, it comes !

O, great good soul of old John Brown,
Through all the land go thundering on,
Till all our armies, all our towns
Shall all be full of brave John Browns,
           Brave John Browns.

OUR DEAD.

OUR graves are strown as seeds are sown,
    From Lapland to Japan,
Where summer wears her broidered zone
On isles so fair they half atone
    For Paradise to man ;

Where cradle breezes rock the palms,
    Some dear ones fell asleep,
Where Burmah's voices swell the psalms,
Or stars shine down the tropic calms
    To double in the deep ;

Where far Nevada's silver shines—
    By Ophir's golden gate—
Where white with snow the emerald pines
Stand sentry on the Arctic lines,
    Some peaceful sleepers wait.

Some camped amid Oneida's Hills,
    Some marked in Federal Blue,
Where battery throbs and bugle thrills
Made pulses leap like mountain rills,
    The iron tempest through.

And the drummers beat the rattling roll
    Where glory kept the gate,
And death took toll of many a soul,
Rent silver cord and golden bowl,
    For death is glory's mate.

Their names are on life's roll to-day,
    We will not bid "Good-night,"
They halt for us beside the way,
We may not mourn, but only say
    "Good morn! 'Tis growing light."

BETWEEN THE CENTURIES.

BY JANE M. READ.

Two men were passing through a village street.
    This one with furrowed brow, long, snow-white
        hair,
And flowing beard, was like the trees we meet
    In dim old forests; trees whose strong trunks
        bear
The marks of storms that beat on them in vain;
For life's rough storms, again and yet again,
Had burst on him, and then had passed away,
Revealing glories of departing day.

That one was proud and dark and full of thought,
    With footstep firm, and eye whose glances
        keen
Would never quail in hours with danger fraught,
    And hand to wield the sword with regal mien.
A heart that faltered but at deeds of wrong,
For truth and right, remaining leal and strong,
Beat in his breast, as beats the surging sea
On the long shore that skirts the rocky lea.

The man of years looked ever on the past,
    And each new scene recalled it to his mind;

The young man's thoughts were on the future
    cast ;
Conversing, thus, the two were oft combined.
They paused at length beside a crystal stream,
And each was silent, busy with his dream.
Some moments passed and then the old man
    spoke,
And words like these upon the stillness broke :—

    " Walking through the quiet street
      That I often wandered down,
    Years ago, with glad young feet,
    When the world seemed fair and sweet,
    Many scenes of old I meet
      In this calm New England town.

    " Pausing by the brooklet's side,
      Where I oft have paused before,
    Narrow, now, the waters glide
    That I thought the rolling tide
    Of a river, vast and wide,
      In the happy days of yore.

    " As the waters onward go,
      Rippling, dashing, whirling, fleet,
    Soft their murmurings whisper, low,
    Stories of the long ago,
    Told in hours that tender glow,
      When the day and evening meet.

    " 'Mid these tales of old, that dart
      Through the brain and pass away,
    One there is with magic art,
    For it speaks, and tells the heart
    How each patriot bore his part
      In our country's new-born day.

" When the brave stood firm and true
    In that time of hope and dread,
Farmers bade their wives adieu,
Left their harvests where they grew,
Waving 'neath the bending blue,
    Marched to war with hurried tread.

" But the folks must eat or die ;
    So the miller stayed at mill,
Ground the corn and wheat and rye.
Yet he murmured with a sigh,
' Others fight !   Why may not I ? '
    Tossed in spirit as the rill.

" Then his wife, courageous, said :
    ' I will tend the mill for thee ;
Thus the hungry shall have bread :
May our Father o'er your head
Watch in love.'   Away he sped,
    Softly saying : ' Pray for me ! '

" Lingering in the door, she stayed
    Till he passed the distant hill
And was hidden in the glade,
Where the strong oak's pleasant shade
Caused the sunlight's gleam to fade ;
    Then she turned her to the mill.

" So the women reaped the grain,
    And the old men bound the sheaves ;
And in sunshine and in rain,
Little children down the lane
Drove the cows safe home again,
    Waving whips with willow leaves.

" Till at last the war was o'er,
    And through valley, over hill,

Joyful marched the troops, and bore
Banners rent, and stained with gore ;
And the miller came once more
Home to Mary and the mill."

He paused, and then resumed in thoughtful tone :
"A hundred years have well-nigh passed away ;
And as those years on swiftest wings have flown,
How much of good has fallen to decay !
The brave firm hearts that fought for truth and
right,
The strong true hands that bore our colours
bright,
The men who toiled to make our freedom sure,
And records left that ever shall endure,
Where, where alas ! are now those heroes brave ?
They're gone as zephyrs gliding o'er the plain ;
Gone to the cold, the dark, the silent grave,
To wake no more at freedom's pleading strain,
Or raise their voice in darker hours of need,
When vice shall thrive in bold and dangerous deed.
True men have saved thee, country of my birth ;
Then weep to lay their cherished forms in earth.

" Ah ! yes, my friend," exclaimed the dark-eyed
youth,
" Let not those deeds be buried in the dust ;
But, still, some hearts there are of changeless truth,
Some precious gems preserved 'mid cankering
rust,
Think not, because the fathers pass from earth,
The sons forget their deeds of lustrous worth.
Now hear the vision I have seen to-day,
While you thus dreamt of scenes long passed
away :

" I gazed upon the streamlet's flow,
　　I heard its ceaseless drone ;
The sunlight gleamed with gentle glow,
And every wavelet whispered low,
　　In soft and singing tone.

" And fast as glides that sparkling crest,
　　My thoughts have drifted fleet ;
Strange fancies rise within my breast,
A thousand dreams, a wild unrest,
　　A sound like tramping feet.

" I know a time of dread draws near ;
　　Low lies the leaden cloud ;
And every heart is filled with fear,
Lest, soon, in gloom, our freedom dear,
　　The darkness may enshroud.

" No hope remains within my heart ;
　　The flesh is faint and frail ;
While, from the noiseless shadows, start,
Wild, chilling doubts that swiftly dart,
　　And cause my cheeks to pale.

" But lo ! one comes and speaks to me ;
　　' Come, follow where I lead.'
We wander over hill and lea,
Through crowded streets, along the sea,
　　Unseen, with silent speed.

" As thus we pass, I see this sight,—
　　That Christians kneel in prayer,
And plead that freedom's hand of might
May bear aloft a fadeless light,
　　Kept by their Father's care.

"And, when the Sabbath evening bell
   Rings out its solemn call,
Those prayers, like waves that landward swell,
The earnest heartfelt pleadings tell
   That come alike from all.

"Then spoke my guide in accents low,
   With sweet and silvery tone :
'Those prayers to God's great throne shall go;
His arm is mightier than the foe ;
   His ear attends each moan.'

"He spoke the clouds crept far away,
   The tempest passed us o'er,
I saw the brooklet's restless play,
And, in the peaceful summer day,
The sun shone forth once more."

In silence, then, they watched the parting smile
   The sun threw backward past the wooded hill;
The gray rocks answered with a blush the while,
   And crimson tints adorned the gliding rill :
The beauty faded, and they turned their feet
As calmly fell the shades of twilight sweet ;
They passed away as men have passed before ;
They came, they paused, and then were seen no
   more.

INDIANS AT THE BLACK HILLS.

BY S. A. J.

"DRIVE them away, or shoot them at bay,
   Like a wild beast in his lair !
Their hills have gold, and the young and old
   Must go, we care not where.

" Let them haste their flight ere they feel our
   might,
   For this is our day and hour ;
They must stand aside till the fair young bride
   Of Destiny wins her dower."

Let the white man pause, though he heeds no
   laws,
   And bate his boastful breath,
As the arrow stays at the mournful gaze
   Of the antelope in death.

While the low sun burns, the red man turns
   To utter a parting word :
" We may yield our right to your greater might,
   But above us reigns one Lord.

" The hunted deer, if pressed too near,
   May turn from the path aside,
And his foe may lean o'er the rocky steep ;
   Alas ! for the fair young bride.

" Is the eagle blind, as the bats that find
   A home in the caverns deep,
That no sign he sees in the bending trees
   Of the storm that his nest shall sweep ?

" Let his guiding wing no fierce brood bring
   To prey on the wounded deer,
Lest the Highest bend His bow to end
   Their lofty and proud career.

" We may pass away as the dying day,
   Or foam from the crested wave,
But think not long will the bitter wrong
   Lie hid in our lonely grave.

"There may be yet, when our sun is set,
　　Some far-off hunting-ground
That we may share ; but where, O where,
　　Will the pale-face then be found ?

" He will call on the hills that now he wills
　　For his own, on his head to fall,
When the righteous King to the light shall bring
　　The deeds and the doom of all."

———

THE TWENTY-SECOND OF FEBRUARY.

BY WILLIAM CULLEN BRYANT.

PALE is the February sky,
　　And brief the midday's sunny hours ;
The wind-swept forest seems to sigh
　　For the sweet time of leaves and flowers.

Yet has no month a prouder day,
　　Not even when the summer broods
O'er meadows in their fresh array,
　　Or autumn tints the glowing woods.

For this chill season now again
　　Brings, in its annual round, the morn
When, greatest of the sons of men,
　　The glorious Washington was born.

Lo, where, beneath an icy shield,
　　Calmly the mighty Hudson flows !
By snow-clad fell and frozen field
　　Broadening the lordly river goes.

The wildest storm that sweeps through space,
  And rends the oak with sudden force,
Can raise no ripple on his face,
  Or slacken his majestic course.

Thus, 'mid the wreck of thrones, shall live
  Unmarrèd, undimmed, our hero's fame,
And years succeeding years shall give
  Increase of honours to his name.

WHITTIER'S HYMN

FOR THE OPENING OF THE CENTENNIAL EXHIBITION.

OUR fathers' God, from out Whose hand
The centuries fall like grains of sand,
We meet, to-day, united, free,
And loyal to our land and Thee,
To thank Thee for the era done,
And trust Thee for the opening one.

Here, where of old, by Thy design,
The fathers spake that word of Thine
Whose echo is the glad refrain
Of rended bolt and fallen chain,
To grace our festal time, from all
The zones of earth our guests we call.

Be with us while the New World greets
The Old World, thronging all its streets,
Unveiling all the triumphs won
By Art or toil beneath the sun ;
And unto common good ordain
This rivalship of hand band rain.

Thou Who hast here in concord furled
The war-flags of a gathered world,
Beneath our western skies fulfil
The Orient's mission of good-will,
And, freighted with love's golden fleece,
Send back the Argonauts of peace.

For art and labour met in truce,
For beauty made the bride of use,
We thank Thee, while withal we crave
The austere virtues strong to save,
The honour proof to place or gold,
The manhood never bought or sold !

O ! make Thou us, through centuries long,
In peace secure, in justice strong ;
Around our gift of freedom draw
The safeguards of thy righteous law,
And, cast in some diviner mould,
Let the new cycle shame the old !

CENTENNIAL HYMN.

BY S. A. J.

LIKE her own royal bird, with its wide-spreading
    pinions,
  Our broad land extendeth from river to sea,
To sunrise and sunset, inviting the nations
    To come 'neath her shadow, and rest and be
      free.

The white sails are coming across the blue waters,
  They gather, a cloud, on our far-reaching
      strand,

The strangers they bear are Thy sons and Thy
    daughters,
  O Maker and Lord of this beautiful land !

When they look on our country, a vast, new
    creation,
  With wonder its greatness and glory to see,
We will show them Thy Gospel and speak of sal-
    vation,
  The gifts that have made us so blest and so
    free.

We will tell them Thy spirit anoints the true
    priesthood,
  That virtue makes him who receives her a king,
That pillars of State are the school and the
    temple
  Which permanent peace and prosperity bring.

Thou hast given us gold as the stones of the
    mountain,
  And knowledge as waters that cover the sea,
Thou hast given Thy love in our hearts a sweet
    fountain,
  And shall not these gifts be devoted to Thee ?

Our vales are exalted, our hills are made lowly,
  The crooked made straight and the rough places
    plain ;
The horses of fire impatient are panting
  To carry the tidings of One that was slain.

When Thy Gospel is borne to each home in our
    nation,
  And children are praising the Saviour's dear
    name,

A song of thanksgiving, as loud as the ocean,
  Shall rise from our people to God and the Lamb.

The light that first came from the East to our
      border,
  And spread o'er our land like a banner un-
      furled,
The light that increases in lustre by giving,
  Shall flow through our Golden Gate over the
      world.

INDEPENDENCE BELL.

HOW THE BELL RANG, JULY 4, 1776.

There was tumult in the city,
  In the quaint old Quaker town,
And the streets were rife with people,
  Pacing restless up and down;
People gathering at the corners,
  Where they whispered each to each,
And their sweat stood on their temples,
  With their earnestness of speech.

As the bleak Atlantic currents
  Lash the wild Newfoundland shore,
So they beat against the State House,
  So they surged against its door;
And the mingling of their voices
  Made a harmony profound,
Till the quiet street of Chestnut
  Was all turbulent with sound.

" Will they do it?" " Dare they do it?"
  "Who is speaking?" "What's the news?"

"What of Adams?"   "What of Carroll?"
   "O! God grant they won't refuse!"
"Make some way there!"   "Let me nearer!
   "I am stifling!"   "Stifle then!
When a nation's life's at hazard
   We've no time to think of men."

So they beat against the portal,
   Man and woman, maid and child;
And the July sun in heaven
   On the crowd looked down and smiled.
The same sun that saw the Spartan
   Shed his patriot blood in vain,
Now beheld the Soul of Freedom,
   All unconquered, rise again!

So they beat against the portal,
   While all solemnly, inside,
The delegates to Congress,
   With but reason for their guide,
O'er a simple scroll debated,
   Which, though simple it might be,
Could shake the cliffs of England
   With the thunder of the Free!

At the portal of the State House,
   Like some beacon in the storm,
Round which waves are wildly beating,
   Stood a slender, boyish form,
With his eyes fixed on the steeple,
   And his ears agape with greed,
To catch the first announcement
   Of the signing of the deed.

Far aloft in that high steeple
   Sat the bellman, old and gray,

He was weary of the tyrant,
   And his iron-sceptred sway !
So he sat, with one hand ready
   On the clapper of the bell,
When his eye could catch the signal,
   The happy news to tell.

See, see ! the dense crowd quivers
   Through all its lengthy line,
As the boy beside the portal
   Hastens forth to give the sign !
With his little hands uplifted,
   Breezes dallying with his hair,
Hark ! with deep, clear intonation,
   Breaks his young voice on the air ;

Hushed the people's swelling murmur,
   Whilst the boy cries joyously :
" Ring, ring !" he shouts, " Ring ! grandpa,
   Ring ! O, ring for Liberty ! "
Quickly, at the given signal,
   The old bellman lifts his hand,
Forth he sends the good news, making
   Iron music through the land !

How they shouted ! What rejoicing !
   How the old bell shook the air,
Till the clang of Freedom ruffled
   The calm-gliding Delaware !
How the bonfires and the torches
   Lighted up the night's repose,
And from the flames, like fabled Phœnix,
   Glorious Liberty arose ;

M

The old State House bell is silent,
   Hushed is now its iron tongue ;
But the spirit it awakened
   Still is living—ever young ;
And when we greet the smiling sunlight,
   On the Fourth of each July,
Let us not forget the bellman,
   Who, betwixt the earth and sky,
Rang out loudly " Independence ! "
   Which, please God, shall never die !

AMERICA'S SECOND CENTENNIAL,

1976.

BY C. THURBER.

ANOTHER century, from God's hand,
Has sifted like a grain of sand,
Since, on our country's hundreth year,
The nations sent their children here
To see what Freedom's sons had done,
And show what victories they had won.

Not one of all that glad array
That gathered then is here to-day ;
New voices shout, new bosoms beat,
New crowds are thronging every street,
And that sweet Quaker bard that sung
Is singing with a heavenly tongue.

The Freedom that our sires proclaimed,
The legal fabric that they framed,
The States of which the tale is told
By stars upon her banner gold,
Are still our joy, our strength, our pride,
More pure, more strong, and multiplied.

Heads, hearts, and hands on every shore
Have been at work as ne'er before,
And feats achieved, and victories won,
And, greater far than all, begun
But ne'er produced, though trying hard,
A sweeter than our Quaker bard.

The sabre's flash and cannon's roar
Is seen and heard, in war, no more,
For Justice' scale, despised so long,
Decide the weight of right and wrong;
And war surrenders, now, to peace,
A richer than a golden fleece.

The patriot, not the partisan,
The hero, sage, the honest man,—
These only rise to power and place,
And knavery dares not show its face
The treasury, howe'er full it be,
Is safe without a lock and key.

So may all lands, from age to age,
Become more pure and great and sage,
That when his trump the Angel blows,
And each to his own homestead goes,
The home he leaves may have become
Sweet, almost, as his heavenly home.

MISCELLANEOUS.

SUNDAY MORNING—THOUGHTS DURING SERVICE.

BY GEORGE A. BAKER.

Too early, of course! How provoking
    I told ma just how it would be :
I might as well have on a wrapper,
    For there's not a soul here yet to see.

There ! Sue Delaplaine's pew is empty—
    I declare if it isn't too bad !
I know my suit cost more than hers did,
    And I wanted to see her look mad.

I do think that sexton's too stupid—
    He's put someone else in our pew—
And the girl's dress just kills mine completely,
    Now what am I going to do?

The psalter, and Sue isn't here yet?
    I don't care, I think it's a sin
For people to get late to service,
    Just to make a great show coming in.

Perhaps she is sick and can't get here—
    She said she'd a headache last night ;
How mad she'll be after her fussing !
    I declare it would serve her just right.

Oh, you've got here at last, my dear, have you ?
    Well, I don't think you need be so proud
Of that bonnet, if Virot did make it,
    It's horrid fast looking and loud.

What a dress ! --for a girl in her senses
    To go on the street in light blue !
And those coat sleeves—they wore them last
        summer,
    Don't doubt, tho', that she thinks they're new.

Mrs. Gray's polonaise was imported—
    So dreadful !—a minister's wife,
And thinking so much about fashion !—
    A pretty example of life !

The altar's dressed sweetly—I wonder
    Who sent those white flowers for the front ?
Some girl who's " gone " on the assistant,
    Don't doubt it was Bessie Lamont.

Just look at her now, little humbug !—
    So devout—I suppose she don't know
That she's bending her head too far over,
    And the ends of her switches all show.

What a sight Mrs. Ward is this morning !
    That woman will kill me some day,
With her horrible lilacs and crimsons.
    Why will these old things dress so gay ?

And there's Jenny Welles with Fred Tracy—
　　She's engaged to him now—horrid thing !
Dear me ! I'd keep on my gloves sometimes.
　　If I did have a solitaire ring !

How *can* this girl next to me act so—
　　The way that she turns round and stares,
And then makes remarks about people ;
　　She'd better be saying her prayers.

Oh dear ! what a dreadful long sermon !
　　He must love to hear himself talk ;
And it's after twelve, how provoking !
　　I wanted to have a nice walk.

Through at last !　Well, it isn't so dreadful
　　After all for we don't dine till one.
How can people say church is poky ?
　　So wicked !—I think it's real fun.

———

A CHICAGO man's young wife entertained him with selections from Wagner, after which he expressed himself as resigned to go to bed, where he slept very soundly. Towards midnight cats assembled in the back-yard, and howled frightfully. The sleeper did not get up and throw boot-jacks at them, but turned on one elbow and whispered in his dreams, " Sing it once more, Elvira ; sing it once more." She sings it no more, nor anything else, but rather thinks of chopping her piano into firewood and turning her music-book into paper-curls.

OUTWITTED.

BY RACHEL POMEROY.

THE Muhlheim monks were jolly and fat—
Trust their larder and pouch for that ;
In many a league you might not see
So opulent a monastery.
Their board was sumptuous every day,
The king in his palace fared plainer than they ;
And as for their cellar, so luscious a hoard
Deep in its fragrant vault was stored,
Some brother at prayer, smacking lips wine-wet—
Half-a-doze—would liker than not forget
To count his rosary bead by bead,
Mumbling the date of a vintage instead.

The monks were wily and hated work,
Drones, agreeing to gorge and shirk ;
Next to their bellies they loved their store ;
Studying always to make it more ;
And ever with all their getting there grew
The fatal lust of adding thereto ,
Greedy and sly ; on every side
Stretched the convent acres wide ;
Yet were not the sluggards satisfied.
Still they ogled with covetings great
Piece of Count Rupert's brave estate—
One hundred acres—a goodly slice
That mightily tickled their avarice.
They raked the records o'er and o'er—
Never had monk so delved before—
Out of their parchments thing to claim

Fraudulent power to clutch the same.
The judges perceived where justice lay,
Yet loth to cross the church were they;
Those being the old-fashioned times, you see,
When facts and piety didn't agree :—
And Rupert was looking with some dismay
To find his inheritance wrenched away;
When lo! on a cunning device he hit,
And my gentlemen monks at the bait-hook bit.
"Give me leave to sow one crop alone,
And harvest the seed when fully grown;
Thereafter, for that ye crave it sore,
I'll give you the land for evermore."
Verily, here was a piece of luck!
The brethren chuckled, the bargain was struck;
And, the surer to clench it in every way,
They drew up a contract that very day,
Which, nice in phrase and legal in plan,
Was signed by monks and by nobleman.
Count Rupert has sowed; they watch to know
What choice of grain the crop may show
Will he wheat, or barley, or oat devise
To deck his land for the sacrifice?
The ground is sprouting with tender green—
Sure never before such grain was seen!
'Tis the seed of oaks—he has planted it thick—
None but the sower of acorns may pick;
The contract hath writ it; 'twas worded plain;
Silly gray cowls, do you dare complain?

Our foxy monks their match had met;
Caught for the nonce in the trap they set.
I trow they never cared again
To play the trick attempted then,

Nor won the prize they coveted ;
For, certes, every soul was dead,
And Rupert himself in the tomb laid down,
Ere his trees to the cloister roof were grown.
And before the oak forest felt decay,
The cloister walls had crumbled away.

THE BELL OF ATRI.

BY HENRY W. LONGFELLOW.

At Atri in Abruzzo, a small town
Of ancient Roman date, but scant renown,
One of those little places that have run
Half up the hill, beneath a blazing sun,
And then sat down to rest, as if to say,
" I climb no further upward, come what may,"—
The Re Giovanni, now unknown to fame,
So many monarchs since have borne the name,
Had a great bell hung in the market-place
Beneath a roof, projecting some small space,
By way of shelter from the sun and rain.
Then rode he through the streets with all his train,
And with the blast of trumpets loud and long,
Made proclamation, that whenever wrong
Was done to any man, he should but ring
The great bell in the square, and he, the King,
Would cause the Syndic to decide thereon.
Such was the proclamation of King John.

How swift the happy days of Atri sped,
What wrongs were righted, need not here be said.
Suffice it that, as all things must decay,
The hempen rope at length was wore away,

Unravelled at the end, and, strand by strand,
Loosened and wasted in the ringer's hand,
Till one, who noted this in passing by,
Mended the rope with braids of briony,
So that the leaves and tendrils of the vine
Hung like a votive garland at a shrine.

By chance it happened that in Atri dwelt
A Knight, with spur on heel and sword in belt,
Who loved to hunt the wild-boar in the woods,
Who loved his falcons with their crimson hoods,
Who loved his hounds and horses, and all sports
And prodigalities of camps and courts ;—
Loved, or had loved them ; for at last, grown old,
His only passion was the love of gold.

He sold his horses, sold his hawks and hounds,
Rented his vineyards and his garden-grounds,
Kept but one steed, his favourite steed of all,
To starve and shiver in a naked stall.
And day by day sat brooding in his chair,
Devising plans how best to hoard and spare.

At length he said : " What is the use or need
To keep at my own cost this lazy steed,
Eating his head off in my stables here,
When rents are low and provender is dear ?
Let him go feed upon the public ways ;
I want him only for the holidays."
So the old steed was turned into the heat
Of the long, lonely, silent, shadeless street ;
And wandered in suburban lanes forlorn,
Barked at by dogs, and torn by briar and thorn.

One afternoon, as in that sultry clime
It is the custom in the summer-time,
With bolted doors and window-shutters closed,
The inhabitants of Atri slept or dozed;
When suddenly upon their senses fell
The loud alarm of the accusing bell!
The Syndic started from his deep repose,
Turned on his couch, and listened, and then rose
And donned his robes, and with reluctant pace
Went panting forth into the market-place,
Where the great bell upon its cross-beam swung,
Reiterating with persistent tongue,
In half-articulate jargon, the old song:
"Some one hath done a wrong, hath done a
      wrong!"

But ere he reached the belfry's light arcade
He saw, or thought he saw, beneath its shade,
No shape of human form of woman born,
But a poor steed, dejected and forlorn,
Who with uplifted head and eager eye
Was tugging at the vines of briony.
"Domeneddio!" cried the Syndic straight,
"This is the Knight of Atri's steed of state!
He calls for justice, being sore distressed,
And pleads his cause as loudly as the best."

Meanwhile from street and lane a noisy crowd
Had rolled together like a summer cloud,
And told the story of the wretched beast
In five-and-twenty different ways at least,
With much gesticulation and appeal
To heathen gods, in their excessive zeal.
The Knight was called and questioned; in reply
Did not confess the fact, did not deny;

Treated the matter as a pleasant jest,
And set at naught the Syndic and the rest,
Maintaining, in an angry undertone,
That he should do what pleased him with his own.

And thereupon the Syndic gravely read
The proclamation of the King ; then said :
" Pride goeth forth on horseback grand and gay,
But cometh back on foot, and begs its way ;
Fame is the fragrance of heroic deeds,
Of flowers of chivalry and not of weeds !
These are familiar proverbs ; but I fear
They never yet have reached your knightly ear.
What fair renown, what honour, what repute,
Can come to you from starving this poor brute ?
He who serves well and speaks not merits more
Than they who clamour loudest at the door.
Therefore, the law decrees that as this steed
Served you in youth, henceforth you shall take
        heed
To comfort his old age, and to provide
Shelter in stall, and food, and field beside."

The Knight withdrew abashed ; the people all
Led home the steed in triumph to his stall.
The King heard and approved, and laughed in
        glee,
And cried aloud : " Right well it pleaseth me !
Church bells at best but ring us to the door ;
But go not in to Mass ; my bell doth more ;
It cometh into court and pleads the cause
Of creatures dumb and unknown to the laws ;
And this shall make, in every Christian clime,
The Bell of Atri famous for all time."

THE TWO ARMIES.

BY O. W. HOLMES.

As life's unending column pours,
  Two marshalled hosts are seen—
Two armies on the trampled shores
  That death flows back between.

One marches to the drum-beat's roll,
  The wide-mouthed clarion's bray,
And bears upon a crimson scroll,
  "Our glory is to slay."

One moves in silence by the stream,
  With sad, yet watchful eyes,
Calm as the patient planet's gleam
  That walks the clouded skies.

Along in front no sabres shine,
  No blood-red pennons wave ;
Its banner bears the single line,
  "Our duty is to save."

For those no death-bed's lingering shade,
  At Honour's trumpet-call,
With knitted brow and lifted blade,
  In glory's arms they fall.

For these no flashing falchions bright,
  No stirring battle cry ;
The bloodless stabber calls by might—
  Each answers, "Here am I !"

For those the sculptor's laurelled bust,
　The builder's marble piles,
The anthems pealing o'er their dust,
　Through long cathedral aisles.

For these the blossom-sprinkled turf
　That floods the lonely graves
When spring rolls in her sea-green surf
　In flowery foaming waves.

Two paths lead upward from below,
　And angels wait above,
Who count each burning lifedrop's flow,
　Each falling tear of Love.

Though from the Hero's bleeding breast,
　Her pulses Freedom drew,
Though the white lilies in her crest
　Sprang from that scarlet dew—

While Valour's haughty champions wait
　Till all their scars are shown,
Love walks unchallenged through the gate
　To sit beside the throne !

MAKING TRACKS.

A light snow had fallen, and the boys desired
to make the most of it. It was too dry for
snow-balling, and not deep enough for coasting.
It did very well to make tracks in.

There was a large meadow near the place where
they were assembled. It was proposed that they
should go to a tree which stood near the centre

of the meadow, and that each one should start from it, and see who could make the straightest track—that is, go from the tree in the nearest approach to a straight line. The proposition was assented to, and they were soon at a tree. They ranged themselves around it, with their backs towards the trunk. They were equally distant from each other. If each had gone forward in a straight line the paths would have been like the spokes of a wheel—the tree representing the hub. They were to go till they reached the boundaries of the meadow, when they were to retrace their steps to the tree.

They did so. I wish I could give a map of their tracks. Such a map would not present much resemblance to the spokes of a wheel.

" Whose is the straightest ? " said James Allison to Thomas Sanders, who was at the tree first.

" Henry Armstrong's is the only one that is straight at all."

" How could we all contrive to go so crookedly, when the ground is so smooth, and nothing to turn us out of our way ? " said Jacob Small.

" How happened you to go so straight ? " said Thomas.

" I fixed my eye on that tall pine tree, on the hill yonder, and never looked away from it till I reached the fence."

" I went as straight as I could, without looking at anything but the ground," said James.

" So did I," said another.

" So did I," said several others.

It appeared that nobody but Henry had aimed at a particular object. They attempted to go

straight without any definite aim.   They failed.
Men cannot succeed in anything good without a
definite aim.   In order to mental improvement
there must be a definite aim.   In order to do
good there must be a definite aim.   General pur-
poses, general resolutions will not avail.   You
must do as Henry did—fix upon something
distinct and definite as an object and go steadily
forward to it.   Thus only can you succeed.

LITTLE WORRIES.

THOUGH many ills may hamper life
    When fortune turns capricious,
The great but nerve us for the strife,
    The small ones make us vicious.
Fierce griefs are soon outstripped by one
    Who through existence scurries ;
It's harder far a race to run
    With nimble " little worries."

A button bids your shirt good-by
    When late for dinner dressing ;
You have a kite you cannot fly,
    And creditors are pressing.
And run to catch—and lose—a train
    (That fatalist of hurries) ;
Your newest hat encounters rain—
    Life's full of " little worries."

From day to day some silly things
    Upset you altogether ;
There's naught so soon convulsion brings
    As tickling with a feather.

'Gainst minor evils let him pray
　Who fortune's favour curries—
For one that big misfortunes slay
　Ten die of " little worries."

THE FARMER FEEDETH ALL.

BY CHARLES G. LELAND.

My lord rides through the palace gate,
My lady sweeps along in state,
The sage thinks long on many a thing,
And the maiden muses on marrying ;
The minstrel harpeth merrily,
The sailor ploughs the foaming sea,
The huntsman kills the good red deer,
And the soldier wars without e'en fear ;
　　But fall to each, whate'er befall,
　　The farmer he must feed them all.

Smith hammereth cherry red the sword,
Priest preacheth pure the Holy Word,
Dame Alice worketh broidery well,
Clerk Richard tales of love can tell,
The tap-wife sells her foaming beer,
Dan Fisher fisheth in the mere,
And courtiers ruffle, strut, and shine,
While pages bring the gascon wine ;
　　But fall to each, whate'er befall,
　　The farmer he must feed them all.

Man builds his castle fair and high,
Wherever river runneth by,
Great cities rise in every land,
Great churches show the builder's hand,

N

Great arches, monuments, and towers,
Fair palaces and pleasing bowers ;
Great work is done, be't here or there,
And when man worketh everywhere ;
But work or rest, whate'er befall,
The farmer he must feed them all.

"THAY AMEN AND THIT DOWN."

UNFORTUNATELY for the Sunday schools, there are a number of middle-aged gentlemen, who, thinking themselves endowed by nature with oratorical ability, visit Sunday schools to display their speech-making qualities. These gentlemen are very properly termed Sunday-school bores, for they bore the children, bore the superintendent, bore the teachers, and bore every person with whom they are thrown in contact.

One of these gentry had a round of four or five schools which he visited regularly, and as regularly bored his hearers, ending invariably with *Amen !*

Visiting one of the schools during his regular rounds, he made his appearance at the superintendent's desk, who felt greatly annoyed, yet, out of courtesy, asked him if he desired to say a few words to the school.

" Wa'al, yes, I'll say just a word or two ! " and straightening himself up, with one hand on the corner of the desk, and the other feeling for pins at the bottom of his vest, he began : " Wa'al, chil'un, the superintendent wants me to speak ta yer ! " and feeling vigorously for pins, " Neow what shall I say—what shall I talk about ? "

A bright little fellow, about four years of age, sitting in the front seat, who evidently had heard the orator before, jumped to his feet and lisped out, loud enough to be heard all over the school-room : "Thay 'Amen,' and thit down!" The speaker collapsed.

THE GOBBLER'S DEATH.

BY DR. BEETLE.

WHAT mean those sobs we hear around ?
    What mean those falling tears ?
'Tis that another turkey dies,
    Though rich and full of years.

The headsman stands with ready axe,
    Beside the cruel block ;
And to this saddest of all scenes
    The little turkeys flock.

" Oh, father turkey, must you die ? "
    His wives and children say ;
" Must we bemoan a gobbler's death
    On each Thanksgiving Day ? "

He makes a gesture to the throng :
    " Would'st shun the dreadful fate
Of me, my sire, and grandsire too ?
    Then heed each thing I state !

" Keep lean, keep thin, my children dear,
    Beware the extra feed !
Beware the kitchen maiden's voice,
    Who calls to scattered seed ! "

Then to the executioner
  He turns a gentle eye :
" 'Tis but a little neck," he says,
  " One stroke—in death I lie ! "

He calmly kneels before the block
  (The crowd give forth a groan) ;
One moment waits, his handk'chief drops,
  The dreadful deed is done.

JACK IN THE PULPIT.

BY JOHN G. WHITTIER.

UNDER the green trees
  Just over the way
Jack in the pulpit
  Preaches to-day ;
Squirrel and song-sparrow,
  High on their perch,
Hear the sweet lily bells
  Ringing to church.

Come hear what his reverence
  Rises to say,
In his queer little pulpit
  This fine Sabbath day.
Fair is the canopy
  Over him seen,
Painted by nature's hand
  Black, brown, and green ;
Green is his pulpit,
  Green are his bands ;
In his queer little pulpit
  The little priest stands.

In black and gold velvet,
　So gorgeous to see,
Comes with his bass voice
　The chorister bee ;
Green fingers playing
　Unseen on wind lyres,
Bird voices singing,
　These are his choirs.
The violets are deacons.
　I know by this sign,
The cups that they carry
　Are purple with wine.
The columbines bravely
　As sentinels stand
On the lookout, with
　All their red trumpets in hand.

Meek-faced anemones,
　Drooping and sad,
Great yellow violets,
　Smiling out glad,
Buttercups' faces,
　Beaming and bright,
Clovers with bonnets,
　Some red, some white ;
Daisies, their fingers
　Half clasped in prayer,
Dandelions, proud of
　The gold of their hair ;
Innocents, children,
　Guileless and frail,
Their meek little faces
　Upturned and pale ;
Wildwood geraniums
　All in their best,

Languidly leaning
   In purple gauze dressed ;
All are assembled
   This sweet Sabbath day,
To hear what the priest
   In his pulpit will say.

Lo, white Indian pipes
   On the green mosses lie ;
Who has been smoking
   Profanely, so nigh ?
Rebuked by the preacher,
   The mischief is stopped,
But the sinners in haste
   Have their little pipes dropped ;
Let the wind with the fragrance
   Of fern and black birch
Blow the smell of the smoking
   Clear out of the church.

So much for the preacher,
   The sermon comes next :
Shall we tell how he preached it,
   And where was the text ?
Alas, like too many
   Grown-up folks who worship
In churches man-builded, to-day,
   We heard not the preacher
   Expound or discuss ;
We looked at the people
   And they looked at us ;
We saw all their dresses,
   Their colours and shapes,
The trim of their bonnets,
   The cut of their capes ;

We heard the wind organ,
The bee and the bird,
But of Jack in the Pulpit
We heard not a word.

THE TWO RIVERS.

BY HENRY WADSWORTH LONGFELLOW.

SLOWLY the hour-hand of the clock moves round;
So slowly that no human eye hath power
To see it move! Slowly in shine or shower
The painted ship above it, homeward bound,
Sails, but seems motionless, as if aground;
Yet both arrive at last; and in his tower
The slumbrous watchman wakes and strikes
the hour,
A mellow, measured, melancholy sound.
Midnight! the outpost of advancing day!
The frontier town and citadel of night!
The watershed of Time, from which the stream
Of Yesterday and To-morrow take their way,
One to the land of promise and of light,
One to the land of darkness and of dreams!

COMMON THINGS.

BY CLARA B. HEATH,

THEY lie around on every side,
For every day some blessing brings,
We look upon them without pride,
For what are they but common things?
So common that we have not known
The loss that we should feel to-day

If they were gathered, one by one,
   And hidden from our sight away.

So common that we use or waste
   As if they were our very own ;
We sweeten this or that to taste,
   And revel in our joys full blown.
We lay them down, or take them up,
   No thankful thought about them clings,
We do not care to fill our cup,
   Life's golden cup, with common things.

We want some rare and precious pet
   That common people cannot buy ;
We want the best that we can get,
   No matter if the price is high.
Our birds are all too commonplace,
   Bring us some foreign one that sings.
Some beauty that our halls would grace ;
   We've had enough of common things !

We want the best the world affords,—
   Pray who should have it if not we ?
We want the gold the miser hoards,
   We want the pearls that gem the sea.
The world moves slow,—we long to fly,
   How many of us sigh for wings !
Yet we should pass them coldly by,
   Were they once classed with common things.

Whatever is most rich and grand,
   Whatever others most desire,
We fain would hold within our hands—
   To things like these our thoughts aspire.

We would have stars to light our way ;
  Our choice of all Dame Fortune brings ;
Let us remember, when we pray,
  That many lack for common things.

THE STUBBORN BOOT.

" Bother !" was all John Clatterby said,
His breath came quick and his cheek was red ;
He flourished his elbows and looked absurd,
While over and over his " Bother !" I heard.

Harder and harder the fellow worked,
Vainly and savagely still he jerked ;
The boot, half on, would dangle and flap—
" Bother !" and then he bursted the strap.

Redder than ever his hot cheek flamed,
Harder than ever he fumed and blamed ;
He wriggled his heel and tugged at the leather
Till knees and chin came bumping together.

" My boy," said I, in a voice like a flute,
" Why not—ahem !—try the mate of that boot
Or the other foot ?"—" I'm a goose," laughed John
As he stood, in a flash, with his two boots on.

      In half the affairs
        Of this busy life
      (As that same day
        I said to my wife)
      Our troubles come
        From trying to put
      The left-hand shoe
        On the right-hand foot ;

Or *vice versa*,
(Meaning reverse, sir),
To try to force,
As quite of course,
Any wrong foot
  In the right shoe
Is the silliest thing
    A man can do.

UNDER THE SNOW.

BEAUTIFUL, beautiful snow!
  Like raiment all spotless and pure,
Enshrouding the emerald garment
  Which nature so gracefully wore.

The buds and blossoms of spring-time,
  Sweet summer, with trailings of light,
The bending harvest of autumn,
  All shrouded with mantles of white.

The leaves of the trees in the forest
  Fell withered and dry to the ground ;
The waters of lake, stream and river,
  Lie chained while the ice-king is crowned.

Cold snow, so icy and chilling,
  What else lieth under the snow,
From our homes and hearts only riven,
  To rest in the darkness below ?

Closed eyelids lie under the snow,
  With fringes of gold and of brown ;
The light went out from beneath them
  And the darkness now presses them down.

Folded hands lie under the snow,
   Their earth-work all finished at last ;
How often we think how we felt them,
   Grow chilly, then cold in our clasp.

Tired feet lie under the snow,
   Grown wearied with wandering all day ;
But they reached the portals at even
   And entered the shining way.

Dead hearts lie under the snow,
   Once bound to our own as by chains ;
They loved us so long and so well ;—
   Their memory only remains.

Beautiful, beautiful snow !
   What lies under the snow to-night ?
A life that will wake into being
   From under the mantle of white.

The buds and blossoms of spring-time,
   Sweet summer, with burdens of bloom,
The bending harvest of autumn,
   Will rise from the dust of the tomb.

The loved and lost who are resting
   Where we laid them with sorrow and pain,
Will only rest till the summons
   Shall bid them come forth again.

And we, sleeping calmly beside them,
   Shall wake at the Master's voice ;
How warm will be every hand-clasp !
   How every heart will rejoice !

Then beautiful, beautiful snow !
  Come down with your garments so white,
And lovingly fold each sweet promise
  Of a future which seemeth so bright,

"KEEP A STIFF UPPER LIP."

BY PHŒBE CARY.

There has something gone wrong,
  My brave boy, it appears,
For I see your proud struggle
  To keep back the tears.
That is right.   When you cannot
  Give trouble the slip,
Then bear it, still keeping
  " A stiff upper lip !"

Though you cannot escape
  Disappointment and care,
The next best thing to do
  Is to learn how to bear.
If when for life's prizes
  You're running, you trip,
Get up—start again,
  " Keep a stiff upper lip.

THE SEED.

The farmer planted a seed,
A little dry, black seed ;
  And off he went to other work—
  For the farmer was never known to shirk—
And cared for what he had need.

The night came, with its dew—
The cool and silent dew ;
  The dawn came and the day,
  And the farmer worked away
At labours not a few.

Home from his work one day—
One glowing summer day—
  His children showed him a perfect flower ;
  It had burst in bloom that very hour ;
How, I cannot say.

But I know if the smallest seed
In the soil of love be cast,
  Both day and night will do their part ;
  And the sower who works with a trusting heart
Will find the flower at last.

COURAGE TO DO RIGHT.

WE may have courage, all of us,
  To start at honour's call,
To meet a foe, protect a friend,
  Or face a cannon-ball ;
To show the world one hero lives,
  The foremost in the fight—
But do we always manifest
  The courage to do right ?

To answer No ! with steady breath,
  And quick, unfaltering tongue,
When fierce temptation, ever near,
  Her syren song has sung ;

To care not for the bantering tone,
  The jest, or studied slight ;
Content if we can only have
  The courage to do right.

To step aside from Fashion's course,
  Or custom's favoured plan ;
To pluck an outcast from the streets,
  Or help a fellow-man ?
If not, then let us nobly try,
  Henceforth, with all our might,
In every case to muster up
  The courage to do right.

BONE, AND SINEW, AND BRAIN.

BY JOHN BOYLE O'REILLY.

YE white-maned waves of the Western sea,
  That ride and roll to the strand ;
Ye strong-winged birds, never forced alee
  By the gales that sweep toward land !
Ye are symbols of death and of hope that saves,
  As ye swoop in your strength and grace,
As ye roll to the land like the billowed graves
  Of a past and puerile race !

Cry " Presto, change ! " and the lout is lord,
  With his vulgar blood turned blue ;
Go dub your knight with a slap of a sword,
  As the kings of Europe do ;
Go grade the lines of your social mode,
  As you grade the palace wall ;
The people for ever to bear the load
  And the gilded vanes o'er all.

But the human blocks will not lie as still
   As the dull foundation stones ;
But will rise like a sea with an awful will,
   And engulf the golden thrones.
For the days are gone when a special race
   Took the place of the gilded vane ;
And the merit that mounts to the highest place
   Must have bone, and sinew, and brain !

Let the cant of "the march of mind" be heard—
   Of the time to come when Man
Shall lose the mark of his brawn and beard
   In the future's levelling plan.
'Tis the dream of a mind effeminate,
   The whine for an easy crown ;
For there is no meed for the good and great
   In the weakling's levelling down.

A nation's boast is a nation's bone,
   As well as its might of mind ;
And the culture of either of these alone
   Is the doom of a nation signed.
But the cant of the ultra-suasion school
   Unsinews the hand and thigh,
And preaches the creed of the weak to rule,
   And the strong to struggle and die.

Our schools are pressed to the fatal race,
   As if health were the nation's sin,
Till the head grows large, and the vampire face
   Is gorged on the limbs so thin.
Our women have entered the abstract fields,
   And avaunt with the child and home !
While the rind of science a pleasure yields,
   Shall they care for the lives to come ?

And they ape the manners of manly times
  In their sterile and worthless life,
Till the man of the future augments his crimes
  With a raid for a Sabine wife!

Ho! white-maned waves of the Western sea,
  That ride and roll to the strand!
Ho! strong-winged birds, never blown alee
  By the gales that sweep toward land!
Ye are symbols both of a hope that saves—
  As ye swoop in your strength and grace,
As ye roll to the land like the billowed graves
  Of a suicidal race!
Ye have hoarded your strength in its equal parts,
  For the men of the future reign
Must have faithful souls and kindly hearts,
  And bone, and sinew, and brain.

BETTER WHISTLE THAN WHINE.

As I was taking a walk early in December, I
noticed two little boys on their way to school.
The smaller one tumbled and fell, and, though
he was not very much hurt, he began to whine
in a babyish way—not a regular roaring boy-
cry, as though he were half-killed, but a little
cross whine. The older boy took his hand in a
kind and fatherly way, and said: "Oh, never
mind, Jimmy; don't *whine;* it is a great deal
better to *whistle.*" And he began in the merriest
way a cheerful boy whistle. Jimmy tried to join
in the whistle. "I can't whistle as nice as you,
Charlie," said he; "my lips won't pucker up
good." "Oh, that is because you have not got all

the whine out yet," said Charlie : " but you try a
minute, and the whistle will drive the whine
away." So he did, and the last I saw or heard
of the little fellows, they were whistling away as
earnestly as though that were the chief end of
life. I learned a lesson which I hope I shall not
soon forget, and it called out these few lines,
which may possibly cheer another whiner of
mature years, as this class is by no means con-
fined to the children :—

" It is better to whistle than whine ;
    It is better to laugh than to cry,
For though it be cloudy, the sun will soon
        shine
    Across the blue, beautiful sky.

" It is better to whistle than whine.
    Oh man with the sorrowful brow !
Let the words of the child scatter murmurs of
        thine,
    And gather his cheerfulness now.

" It is better to whistle than whine.
    Poor mother ! so weary with care,
Thank God for the love and the peace that are
        thine,
    And the joy of thy litttle ones share.

" It is better to whistle than whine.
    Through troubles you find in your way,
Remember that wise little fellow of mine,
    And whistle *your* whining away.

O

"God bless that brave boy for the cheer
    He brought to this sad heart of mine ;
When tempted to murmur, that young voice I
        hear,
    It is better to whistle than whine ! "

CHERRIES.

UNDER the tree the farmer said,
Smiling and shaking his wise old head :
"Cherries are ripe ! but then, you know,
There's the grass to cut and the corn to hoe ;
We can gather the cherries any day ;
But when the sun shines we must make our hay ;
To-night, when the chores have all been done,
We'll muster the boys for fruit and fun."

Up in a tree a robin said,
Perking and cocking his saucy head :
" Cherries are ripe ! and so, to-day,
We'll gather them while you make the hay ;
For we are the boys with no corn to hoe,
No cows to milk and no grass to mow."
At night the farmer said : " Here's a trick !
Those roguish robins have had their pick."

CLEAR THE WAY.

MEN of thought ! be up and stirring
        Night and day :
Sow the seed—withdraw the curtain—
        Clear the way !

Men of action, aid and cheer them,
  As ye may !
There's a fount about to stream,
There's a light about to beam,
There's a warmth about to glow,
There's a flower about to blow ;
There's a midnight blackness changing
  Into grey !
Men of thought and men of action,
  Clear the way !

Once the welcome light has broken,
  Who shall say
What the unimagined glories
  Of the day ?
What the evil that shall perish
  In its ray ?
Aid the dawning, tongue and pen
Aid it, hopes of honest men ;
Aid it, paper—aid it, type—
Aid it, for the hour is ripe ;
And our earnest must not slacken
  Into play.
Men of thought and men of action,
  Clear the way !

Lo ! a cloud's about to vanish
  From the day ;
And a brazen wrong to crumble
  Into clay.
Lo ! the right's about to conquer—
  Clear the way !

With the Right shall many more
Enter smiling at the door ;

With the giant Wrong shall fall
Many others great and small,
That for ages long have held us
    For their prey.
Men of thought and men of action,
    Clear the way!

www.ingramcontent.com/pod-product-compliance
Lightning Source LLC
Chambersburg PA
CBHW020621030726
47497CB00007B/2354